LISTENING TO PARENTS: An Approach to the Improvement of Home/School Relations

Janet Atkin and John Bastiani (with Jackie Goode), School of Education, University of Nottingham

Positive interaction between home and school in education is currently receiving attention from politicians, parents and teachers. By listening to parents, teachers may gain insight into the ways in which they can work more effectively with children and their families.

This book is of great practical value. It draws upon the authors' work over the last decade to explore the links between listening to the parental perspective on a child's schooling and the development of more effective home/school practice. It describes the current scene, the philosophy and method for effective listening, the development of familiarity and understanding with parents, strategies for encouraging a home/school programme and the development of effective practice. Included are accounts by parents with widely differing backgrounds and experiences on their role as educators and their dealings with their children's schools. The book concludes with a discussion of the important issues in home/school interaction and identification of the areas where further development is needed.

LISTENING TO PARENTS

An Approach to the
Improvement of Home/School Relations

JANET ATKIN and JOHN BASTIANI
(with JACKIE GOODE)

CROOM HELM
London • New York • Sydney

© 1988 J. Atkin, J. Bastiani and J. Goode
Croom Helm Ltd, Provident House,
Burrell Row, Beckenham, Kent BR3 1AT

Croom Helm Australia, 44–50 Waterloo Road,
North Ryde, 2113, New South Wales

Published in the USA by
Croom Helm
in association with Methuen, Inc.
29 West 35th Street
New York, NY 10001

British Library Cataloguing in Publication Data

Atkin, Janet
    Listening to parents: an approach to the
    improvement of home/school relations.
    1. Home and school — Great Britain
    I. Title II. Bastiani, John
    371.1'03'0941   LC225.33.G7

    ISBN 0-7099-5039-X
    ISBN 0-7099-5137-X Pbk

Library of Congress Cataloging-in-Publication Data

Atkin, Janet, 1939–
    Listening to parents: an approach to the improvement of
home/school relations/Janet Atkin and John Bastiani with Jackie
Goode.
        p. cm.
    "Published in the USA by Croom Helm in association with Methuen,
Inc." — T.p. verso.
    Bibliography: p.
    ISBN 0-7099-5039-X. ISBN 0-7099-5137-X (pbk.)
    1. Home and school — Great Britain. 2. Parent-teacher
relationships — Great Britain. I. Atkin, Janet, 1939–
II. Bastiani, John. III. Goode, Jackie. IV. Title.
LC225.33.G7A85   1988
370.19'.31 — dc 19   87-27251

Filmset by Mayhew Typesetting, Bristol, England
Printed and bound in Great Britain
by Billing & Sons Limited, Worcester.

Contents

Preface

This book is part of a long and continuing process of developing our thinking and practice in the area of home/school relations. Our interest was initially prompted in the heady days of the late 1960s when the Plowden Report firmly placed parents upon the agenda of education matters. Since then, as parents ourselves, and as teachers and lecturers, we have lived through the momentary heyday of the James Report and the White Paper of 1972 when all seemed possible in the world of education; we have witnessed the contraction of resources, the growth of unemployment, the Great Debate, the accountability movement and the growing importance of school governors; we have seen the role of parents in education move from the very margin to the centre of the arena. During these years we have worked with both teachers and parents developing and refining our ideas about relationships between homes and schools, and throughout this work we have emphasised the idea that listening to the parental voice is fundamental to the process of developing more effective practice.

The last twenty years have seen many changes in society and in education and the voices of parents are not the same now as when we began our work. For this reason we do not see our book as a definitive statement about home/school relations; rather it is illustrative of the particular approach we have developed, one which we believe is responsive to change.

We could not have formulated our ideas without the help of many people and in particular we would like to thank:

The Community Education Working Party (a group of teachers who worked with us for over a decade at the School of Education, University of Nottingham).

The many teachers who have come to our workshops, invited us to their schools, tried out our ideas and given us many in return.

The parents we interviewed and worked with, who gave us their time so generously.

The Social Science Research Council (now the Economic and Social Science Research Council) for the studentship which enabled Jackie Goode to join us.

The Schools Council (now Schools Curriculum Development Committee) and the School of Education, University of Nottingham for financial support.

John Bird, Headteacher of Meadow Farm Primary School for allowing us to use school material; Helen Astill and Debbie Watchorn for some of the illustrations.

Jill Cleaver, last but definitely not least, our secretary for many years, who has been a loyal friend and patient decipherer of manuscripts.

Introduction

Whilst there has been a widespread increase of interest and activity in the field of home/school relations in recent years, most of it suffers from one particular weakness. For most of the work concerning relations between families and schools is viewed entirely from professional perspectives, through the eyes of schools and teachers and on their terms, rather than those of parents and children.

The present account, by contrast, is a deliberate attempt to redress the balance by providing a stage for the exploration of *parental* perspectives and experience. By drawing from our own thinking and practical work over the last decade, we have tried to create an opportunity for the reader to listen to the rich and varied voices of parents, as they recount their dealings with their children's schools in their own words, before we go on to explore some of the consequences of what they are saying for practising teachers. For we have come to believe that the process of 'listening to parents' should be a crucial element in any attempt to improve home/school relations and is an invaluable source of many ideas for its practical development. So, for us, 'listening to parents' has become not only a cornerstone in our home and school philosophy, but a very productive way of working for schools and teachers.

At the same time, there are certain things that we have deliberately avoided doing. Unlike most books in the home/school field, for instance, we have avoided offering a potted history of the area or a comprehensive overview of the literature. Other people have done this (as we have ourselves on another occasion, in the form of an introductory study guide) and it would interfere with our main purpose. For a similar reason, we have not felt it necessary to argue a detailed case for 'better' home/school relations, for a number of recent accounts have done this thoroughly and well. The justification for developing home/school communication and involvement has also been given a massive boost by accounts which have demonstrated, in a totally convincing way, the tangible benefits of doing so. The involvement of parents in their children's reading, for example, has done more to justify and support a commitment to improving home/school relations than anything in its previous history.

Both of these omissions are part of our deliberate intention to avoid, as far as possible, writing a book that is a standard academic text. For we are not writing to impress the academic world, but to share our thinking and experience in an area which we think is important and which, despite the lip-service paid to it, deserves to be taken more seriously by the education service. So we have tried to avoid some of the more off-putting features of academic approaches, such as larding the text with heady references and epic bibliographies (although we have made *some* suggestions for further reading), and have tried to produce a clear guide that will be of value to hard-pressed teachers.

The structure and organisation of this book is, as far as is possible, based upon the need to demonstrate the value of listening to parents, as a tool in the improvement of home/school relations, for practising teachers. This is not in the form of a theory/practice divide, which has no place in our work, but as a working-through of a research and development process which we have found to be, with common-sense adaptation, entirely suitable to the lives of practising teachers.

In Part One we have attempted to locate our work both against a number of contemporary issues and concerns and in relation to a number of different perspectives on the study and practice of home/school relations. Several of the shared concerns of major interest groups in the field are identified, alongside a number of issues and concerns which are currently attracting a great deal of attention within the educational service. This is followed by a brief look at some of the difficulties in studying home/school thinking and practice in a more-or-less systematic way, with a consideration of some of the characteristic features of home/school issues and practices. The first Part ends with a brief look at some of the beliefs and values which, taken together, constitute something of a 'parent-centred' philosophy, suggesting a rather different basis on which professionals in the health, education and welfare services, might work more effectively with parents and families.

In the second, rather substantial Part, we have provided extended and varied opportunities to 'listen to parents', as they talk reflectively about their dealings with their children's schools and their own roles as parents and educators. This picture of parental perspectives and experience is drawn from a number of different studies which we have carried out and is based upon a broad cross-section of parental attitude, background and experience. It is organised around a number of key themes and processes, some of which will be already familiar to practising teachers, others less so.

Part Three attempts to identify, and work through, the implications of listening to parents for teachers, to find ways of making schools more responsive to what they are saying and to suggest ways of developing appropriate forms of practical action. It begins with the consideration of a number of general issues that relate not only to *what* teachers might consider and do, but also to *how* they might go about it. It then goes on to consider, in a critical way, some of the challenges and problems in the formulation of home/school policies, of planning and evaluation, and in the development of appropriate strategies and resources.

The focus then shifts to a rather more detailed examination of some of the crucial moments in the educational lives of pupils, teachers and parents, together with a consideration of some of the key forms of communication, contact and involvement, particularly as they affect the lives of ordinary teachers.

In Part Four we switch to a wider view, to examine a number of issues and areas of development which are of concern to the education service as a whole. This begins by returning to the arena of educational politics, as it concerns the formulation of policy, the allocation of resources and the development of practice. Finally, we have identified a number of implications for training and professional development, together with some basic suggestions for an appropriate approach.

Part One

Listening to Parents: The Background

1

The Current Scene

In recent years the study and practice of home/school relations, with its characteristic issues and problems, have received increasing attention. This is largely because a number of its central concerns figure prominently on the agendas of politicians, professionals and parents alike, albeit in a different ways.

For *politicians* have come to recognise parents as an important lobby, a key sounding-board for proposed policies and an important source of electoral support. Currently, such an interest can be located against the background of a commitment to reduce public expenditure, to get better value for money from public services and to make educational institutions more accountable to public pressure. Politicians from all parties, however, have been quick to seize upon public anxieties about the standards of performance in our schools, which have been fuelled by the media rather than grounded in evidence.

Characteristically, governments have tended to see home/school matters in terms of policy and legislation rather than, for example, the development of 'good practice', which focuses on the actual dealings between teachers and parents. So contemporary education acts have attempted to chart something of parental rights and obligations in this area, as they concern a particular notion of parental choice, and to support processes of communication and consultation. Most recently, legislation has give parents a bigger formal stake in the management of their children's schools.

For *professionals* working in the education service, parents can be seen to have moved, as a result of their own and the government's efforts, from a shadowy position on the margins of the educational process to a position nearer the centre of the stage. Although this has not necessarily been greeted with wild enthusiasm by all teachers, the crucial influence of parents upon their children's education and development is at last being widely recognised, however reluctantly. Although a steady accumulation of research evidence and professional development has put this beyond reasonable doubt, it mainly serves to confirm what many teachers know in their bones, as the result of their daily experience in classrooms.

Increasingly, too, teacher/parent relationships have been the object of serious consideration by a number of different groups within the education system. Teacher associations have issued discussion documents and have attempted to provide guidelines; a few local authorities have issued recommendations and suggestions for practice in a number of appropriate areas and a small, but important, number of home/school projects have published their experience. Above all, a steadily increasing number of individual schools seem to focus at least some of their attention and in-service efforts on the improvement of their home/school activities. As a result of this combined attention, a number of discussion and policy statements have emerged, in which uplifting rhetoric about 'partnership' is tempered by strong reservations about increasing demands upon teachers beyond reasonable limits.

Most recently, the prolonged dispute between the government and the teaching profession, in which parents have played an important role, has brought to a head a number of unresolved issues concerning the nature of teachers' duties and performance. Amongst such issues figure the nature of contractual versus voluntary obligations and the answerability of schools to the outside world in general, and to parents in particular. Although it is very difficult to say what the long-term effects of such a conflict will be, it is clear that its central problems will need to be resolved sooner or later.

For *parents*, the last decade has seen slow but unspectacular progress in combating the notion that their children's education was 'not really any of their business' or that their contact with their children's schools should be very limited, except as fund-raisers or extra pairs of hands in an emergency. By getting more organised, in national and local groups, parents have been able to exert a steady pressure upon schools and the system, to oblige them to recognise parental rights and expectations and to become more responsive to their needs and interests.

More recently, the focus of parental anxiety and concern has shifted from the alleged inadequacies of the teaching profession, the breakdown of teacher authority or the incomprehensibility of modern teaching methods (often hyped-up by press and television), towards a growing concern about the quality of provision in their children's schools, in such areas as staffing levels, the condition of buildings and the provision of equipment.

So home/school relations have become firmly established as an important area of contemporary concern for politicians, professionals and parents alike, although their viewpoints and experience can be *very* different. Shared concerns, however, have focused attention upon a number of recurring topics such as the preferences of parents for particular forms of education and their expectations of their children's schools or the nature of teacher and parent contributions to the educational process, together with a clearer understanding of the obligations and responsibilities of each.

As part of the current scene, both the study and practice of home/school relations are centrally concerned with a number of overlapping issues which run throughout this account. These focus upon the formulation of policy and the subsequent allocation of resources, the identification of important areas for research and development, management and evaluation issues and their implications for teacher training and professional development.

In addition to these, the current home/school scene picks up and reflects back a number of the more general, widely held concerns in the broader field of education and social policy. These currently include:

- the performance of schools and their accountability to external audiences;
- the management of educational institutions and processes;
- the meeting of special needs: policy, provision and practice;
- education in multicultural settings;
- co-operation between different agencies concerned with the health, education and welfare of children and young people.

Both sets of issues, the specific and the more general, are increasingly likely to be explored against the background of a wider debate about the nature of teachers' contractual obligations and professional responsibilities.

Home/school relations take place against a broader backcloth of social and educational change, and owe as much to the persistence of some old problems as to the emergence of some of the new and far-reaching changes that are currently taking place. Parents, for example, could easily be forgiven for continuing to believe that school leavers need a GCSE to breathe, let alone become a reasonably

5

well-adjusted, employable adult. For the need to obtain qualifications through formal educational achievement, in a competitive environment, continues to operate a vice-like grip, which filters right down through the system. Similarly, although some classrooms are still heavily reminiscent of neolithic life or the Bash Street Kids, the vast majority of schools and classrooms *have* changed, certainly since most parents were pupils themselves. The cumulative effect of such change is to present enormous obstacles of communication and understanding which, if ignored or unresolved, inevitably heighten anxiety and frustration amongst parents, or even lead to open conflict.

There have also been important and widespread changes in the structure and organisation of both family and community life. Arrangements for bringing up children are now very diverse, as class teachers and form tutors are constantly finding out, with widely differing values and styles of parenting associated with such a task. These are also reflected in the changing faces and lifestyles of neighbourhoods, particularly in our large cities. Taken together, these changes represent a shifting pattern in the relationships between the major institutions of family, school and work, whose effects are felt, often painfully, by institutions and individuals alike. Such a shift also represents a series of both challenges and opportunities. From whatever angle you look at it, one thing is clear. There has never been a greater need for schools and families to co-operate and, where possible, to support one another, in the interests of the children for whom they are both responsible, albeit in different ways.

Although it has taken a long time to become recognised, the case for 'better' home/school relations can be firmly based and strongly supported. For what originally began as an act of faith on the part of a committed minority, can now be seen as an important consideration in the relationship between *all* schools and their communities. Getting all teachers to accept this, or finding ways of translating its goals into effective, practical action is, of course, another matter.

Although we have decided to avoid making a detailed 'case' for the improvement of home/school relationships it is necessary to acknowledge the view that the effective education of the next generation requires us to recognise the *needs, wishes and experience* of children and their families. Put another way, it is both an educational and a professional nonsense for schools (or individuals within them) to operate in ignorance of, and isolation from, the families they serve and the neighbourhoods in which they have been located.

Such a claim has considerable roots in evidence and experience. More recently, it has been possible to show, sometimes dramatically, that when parents

- understand what the school is trying to do,
- identify with its main goals and support its efforts,
- understand something of their role as educators,
- take an active interest in, and provide support for, their children's school work,

then the effects can be both dramatic and long-lasting.

Again, whether we like it or not, current opinion recognises that parents have *rights* in their children's schooling, as well as obligations. It is necessary to say it is now the 'official' view that parents are entitled to opportunities to be consulted about, and participate in, the education and development of their children. The opposite side of this particular coin is that schools also need the active and continuing *support* of their parents — not just as long pockets or unpaid helpers — but for the central educational tasks and responsibilities which are their main concern. There is a great deal that parents know and can do, particularly with regard to their own children. This makes them a vitally important and potentially valuable *resource*, which most schools do not even recognise, let alone utilise effectively.

Perhaps such ideas sound too lofty and need to be countered with doses of realism and expediency. For families and schools have much to offer each other of a down-to-earth, practical and utilitarian nature and it is not surprising that, when schools attempt to improve their work with parents, they seldom have regrets or wish to turn the clock back. There is certainly no room for complacency and plenty for honest self-criticism. For there is still plenty of evidence of schools that fail to keep parents informed, of parental anxieties that go unrecognised or of home and school continuing to harbour gross misconceptions about each other. So, whilst there has been steady progress in recent years and much valuable thinking and improved practice, there is still a long way to go.

2

The Examination of Home/School Issues

The study of home/school matters is rapidly coming of age. For significant changes are now taking place both in the conventional wisdom and in widely accepted practice; new perspectives, which give rise to very different views of the key issues and problems, are emerging, and call for different methods of study and inquiry; above all, the critical examination of home/school matters is increasingly felt to make a useful contribution to the development of both thinking and practice and to be an important ingredient in the professional development of teachers in this area. All of this makes the study of relations between families and schools, between teachers, parents and pupils, a particularly relevant and challenging task for those who currently work with children and young people.

In the past, the study of home/school relations appears to have followed three rather narrow and separate tracks, each with its own characteristic approaches, literature and followers. Firstly, there was an extensive *research* tradition, which grew strong in conjunction with the emergence of education as a public service in post-war Britain. It was part of a wider commitment to an ideology of equality of opportunity and to the development of the welfare state, beliefs whose self-evident importance has certainly been under attack in recent years.

Given the profound changes of social and political attitude that appear to have taken place in the last decade, it would be all too easy to dismiss this work as hopelessly idealistic attempts to improve society through social engineering, which were bound to fail. However, such research has done a great deal to highlight educational problems that are based upon persistent inequalities of family, class and background, and to pinpoint areas of social and educational need. Research cannot be held responsible for the failure of politicians and others to act upon the findings, however convincing they appear to be!

The second tradition in the study of home/school relations has grown not so much out of educational practice as out of its *rhetoric*. Accounts about 'the way things *should* be' were particularly influential during the late sixties and early seventies. These could be located against a background influenced by the rapid expansion of the teaching profession and its developing professionalism (and the associated problems of providing appropriate training and support), together with a growing public interest in education and a belief in its value, both instrumentally in terms of securing jobs and in its power to enrich the lives of individuals. How the world has changed!

Typically, accounts of this kind, which are often written by practitioners who have been elevated to the peerage, such as retired headteachers, advisers, etc., are usually restricted to the level of common-sense, practical advice. Their tone is uplifting, if somewhat idealistic, and they tend to play down both actual and imagined problems in a desire to please everyone. In such accounts there is hardly ever any theoretical point of reference or any real empirical support based upon other people's work and experience.

The third component of home/school relations as a field of study derives from the actual *practice* of schools and the actual dealings of teachers, parents and pupils with each other. Although very much neglected and underdeveloped, the examination of home/school matters has increasingly given much greater emphasis to the desirability of obtaining an empirical base against which issues can be analysed and policies formulated. This is particularly important in an area where the rhetoric has been dominant and where it would be all too easy to confuse what people think *should* be happening with what is actually taking place.

The uneven and patchy availability of empirical evidence also owes something to the widespread failure to acknowledge openly the rather shadowy and ambiguous place of home/school relationships and responsibilities in the professional lives of teachers. There is almost nothing that is explicit in teacher' contracts, in DES or LEA regulations or in most school-based policies that spells out the nature and extent of their duties towards parents and families, a situation recognised by both sides in disputes involving teachers and their employers.

This apparent lack of official professional commitment has often been matched, for parents, by a correspondingly low threshold of expectation of rights concerning their children's schooling, or by the lack of a clear understanding of how to behave. Wide differences of belief and practice, reinforced by the absence of formal rules, have characterised the behaviour of parents and teachers alike, and influenced the majority of their dealings with each other. Against such a background, current developments can be seen as both challenging and wide-ranging.

THE 'PROBLEMATIC' NATURE OF HOME/SCHOOL RELATIONS

Until a few years ago, the study and practice of home/school relationships was not really given a great deal of serious attention. It might be seen as a rather distant concern of planners and government researchers, taking a broader view of family, school, work relationships; it was established as a minor topic about which teachers in training wrote flabby essays after a couple of lectures on social background and educational achievement; as an applied area it was assumed that teachers learned how to 'handle' parents as a matter of course, naturally, alone and unaided, in the fullness of time. For schools and practising teachers, however, it was regarded as an optional extra, to be taken up or ignored according to personal philosophy or experience: what teachers believed and what they did, in respect of parents, was felt to be *their* prerogative.

Underlying such a view is a series of assumptions, shared by teachers and parents alike, about the way the world is, and is likely to continue to be. More recently much of this 'taken-for-granted' wisdom has been firmly questioned, often with profound and far-reaching implications for thinking and practice in this area. Here are some examples:

(a) Many home/school issues are not nearly as straightforward as they at first appear to be — there's more to them than meets the eye! For example, teacher/parent interaction is often accounted for in terms of two major sets of views — those of teachers and those of parents. This ignores crucially important and wide-ranging differences *within* the teaching profession and *amongst* parents. There are many issues like this, where the basic assumptions need to be examined against an understanding of the real world that incorporates evidence about what makes things tick.

When it comes to it most of us, teachers and parents alike, are in favour of 'better' relationships with each other. The problem lies in deciding what that means! Any idea, for example, that there is a blueprint for perfect relationships or a panacea for all ills, is naïve, unhelpful and, in the end, self-defeating. For in the real world, it is much easier to make claims about progress or greater satisfaction in our work than it is to substantiate them.

Improvements can often be blurred or disguised, or take longer to appear than we had allowed for; so often development and change appear to have produced a new set of problems to replace those we thought we had come to terms with or even resolved. It's not difficult to see, for example, how the opening up of public institutions like schools and the increasing co-operation and involvement of parents is bound to make new demands, to create different tensions and to bring new problems. Yet it is surprising how often this is suppressed or ignored in the plans we make and the work we do.

(b) Despite the cosy and uplifting rhetoric about 'partnership' and 'co-operation' and the spread of 'good practice', home/school relationships in the real world are just as much characterised by underlying tension and intractable dilemmas. At the heart of the business of schooling are processes which contrast sharply with some of the key features of family life. The crowded nature of classroom life and the competitive nature of schooling illustrate the potential for disagreement and conflict. Schools can be harsh worlds to inhabit and the scramble for achievement and success divides parents as surely as it divides pupils. Families and schools are *very* different kinds of institutions. Although there is common ground, they have their own, sometimes contradictory, concerns and responsibilities. Most home/school accounts contain absolutely no inkling of any of this!

(c) In their dealings with their children's schools, many parents encounter a system that 'speaks with forked tongue'! For home/school relations, like much educational and social life, are an area where our fine words and our actions do not always match up. Here, as elsewhere, we do not always practise what we preach, neither do our good intentions always lead to effective action; the relationship between rhetoric and practice is not always either close or consistent.

(d) Above all, much of the thinking and practice in the field of home/school relations is characterised by a number of unchallenged assumptions about professional knowledge and authority. It is only when one begins to examine the basis of professional expertise from a different angle, and from a different values-position, that the

11

dominance of professional perspectives and attitudes in education (and in other areas of professional life) becomes clear.

However, these forms of professional dominance *are* being challenged, in theory and in practice, and their consideration provides the basis of an alternative philosophy, which underpins much of the present account and provides a great deal of its distinctive approach and flavour.

A PARENT-CENTRED RATIONALE

Whilst it cannot be easily defined, a 'parent-centred' philosophy can be seen as having a number of distinct, though overlapping, purposes which have rather different implications for thinking and practice:

(1) The careful and systematic consideration of the *experience* of parents, and other client groups, should be a crucial ingredient in the appraisal and evaluation of public services, particularly in the fields of health, education and welfare. Such consideration needs to go beyond matters of provision and access, to consider both the needs of clients, as they perceive them, and their assessment of the quality of their current experience.

(2) As consumers of public services, parents (and others, including children and young people themselves) have important *rights* and *obligations*. In recent years, supported by a series of reports sponsored by successive governments (Plowden; Court; Taylor; Warnock), it has become increasingly accepted that parents should be consulted about, and involved with, processes that deeply affect both the shorter- and longer-term development of their children.

(3) There is growing acceptance of, and support for, the view that when professionals and parents share some of the same goals and work together in an *active partnership*, things can really begin to happen! A most striking contemporary example, which can draw upon powerful evidence from Haringey, Coventry, Sheffield and elsewhere, concerns the involvement of parents in their children's reading. For the evidence shows conclusively that where parents and teachers work together, the gains that children make are both dramatic and sustainable, even when those children have started from a position of serious under-achievement.

Such encouraging experience, based upon new kinds of teacher/

parent partnerships, is becoming more widespread in other areas and can be found in the pre-school world, elsewhere in the formal education system, in social work, youth and community work and in the work of the health and welfare services. It also appears likely to survive the influence of contrary forces, of accelerating centralism and inimical government policies and shrinking resources.

(4) Parents (although the same is true of other 'client groups' such as claimants, patients, etc.) possess crucially important knowledge and experience, which not only complements that of professionals but is valuable in its own right. In educational terms, parents are an essential *resource* and also have unique opportunities as educators — a powerful combination.

Whilst such an argument has long had a place in the rhetoric of home/school relationships and in the field of community education, it has not yet acquired a clear place in the everyday assumptions that are made about teaching and learning. Nevertheless, the recognition of the educative elements in communities is an area where progress is being made, in a steady but unspectacular way.

(5) Finally, there is an important element in a parent-centred rationale which is nevertheless very difficult to pin down. It is centrally concerned with *respect for the everyday lives of ordinary people*, both as individuals and in groups, *for its own sake*, and is strongly invested with philosophical, political and moral significance.

Such a value, described as 'autonomy' or 'respect for persons' in education, or 'client self-determination' in social work, is deeply embedded in the rhetoric of caring professions. It is particularly audible during training, though it is more difficult to find in subsequent practice!

These values, and the actions they give rise to, constitute an embryonic form of a very different rationale of professional/client relationships from that which currently prevails in the world of teacher/parent relationships. Embodied within it are a number of implications for policy, training and practice which have influenced our work strongly during the last decade and whose implications we have tried to explore and develop in practical forms, in our work with teachers and parents.

13

3

Listening to Parents — as a Philosophy and a Way of Working

To become obliged to examine the foundations on which one's work and professional interests are based, is a challenging and often uncomfortable business. In our case, it was something that grew steadily for a number of years, for we were already engaged in in-service work in the field of home, school and community. In the early years this consisted largely of the training of home/school liaison teachers, exploring the conventional wisdom about home/school and community education matters and running short, practical workshops in areas like written communication, based on earlier studies which we had carried out. During this period, we became increasingly aware of a number of important deficiencies of perspective and evidence — a sense of pieces that did not fit together satisfactorily — which niggled and would not go away.

In the first place we had become rather suspicious of many of the claims that practising teachers were making about what parents were like. Increasingly, we began to consider that such claims were rooted in teacher lore and staffroom mythology, rather than in first-hand experience and direct evidence, being strongest where actual contact was weak or limited. To this day, we maintain a healthy scepticism about persistent teacher stereotypes of parents, such as 'uninterested' parents, those who 'want to take over', or the view that 'you never see the parents that you really want to see'.

At the same time, we had become more confident in voicing a number of major criticisms of extremely influential studies in the home/school field, such as the Plowden Report, whose findings many later studies had accepted uncritically and amplified in their own work. Much of the collected wisdom, for example, turns out not to be based upon direct evidence obtained from parents themselves, but upon teacher assessments of parental interest and involvement, which is a *quite* different matter.

In a more obviously positive way, our growing experience of working with parents, at different tasks and in different settings, confirmed our belief that there were many things that parents knew and were good at, that were of critical importance in the education of their children. In practice, by contrast, this valuable resource is seldom even recognised by schools and teachers, let alone productively tapped.

Taken together, such criticisms pointed unmistakably in one direction, telling us what we should do next. It became obvious that what we needed (and what was so badly missing elsewhere in the field of home/school relations) was a credible picture of *parental perspectives and experience*, based upon what parents *themselves* told us about their dealings with their children's schools, supplemented, where possible, with other kinds of evidence and experience.

To do this, we carried out a programme of interviews in the homes of a large and very diverse sample of parents. We tried to identify a broad cross-section of parental perspectives by incorporating parents with widely differing attitudes, backgrounds and experience; we deliberately set up contrasts by drawing from different ends of the spectrum of parenting experience and from parents with very different opportunities for contact with different kinds of schools; we were also interested in both the normal, everyday experiences which parents have, as well as the special occasions and circumstances in which home/school matters are experienced in a particular, or heightened, way.

So, from a series of rather vague beliefs about the unacknowledged value of parents in their children's education, together with a number of unresolved criticisms of the study and practice of home/school relations, we set out to 'listen to parents' on a rather grand scale, but in a fairly systematic and down-to-earth way. We had no idea of the extent it was to influence our thinking and our work on a permanent basis. Such a development also had the effect of bringing our work more sharply into focus. We found ourselves, for example, articulating our interests through a number of overlapping themes, which echoed some of the wider issues derived from family/school relationships in a rather special way. These were harnessed to a continuing concern to:

- improve communication and contact between teachers and parents;

- help parents make sense of their children's schooling;
- encourage parents to have more confidence in their own distinctive skills as educators.

Although we have added a number of further concerns to these, they remain the main themes in our exploration of parental attitudes and experience and for the subsequent development of practical initiatives. These themes, which will be recognisable as part of the sub-structure of Part Two of this book, also served to bring together a number of separate activities which led to the formation of 'The Development of Effective Home/School Programmes' Project. This was never a project in the conventional sense, but a coalition of research, study and development work, with no fixed dates for completion and whose overall aim is to bring about improvements in home/school *practice*. Its work has included:

- The publication of reports and INSET training materials in such contrasting areas as written communication and face-to-face contact between teachers and parents. These have been supported by a series of practical, two-day workshops.
- The development of taught courses which encourage teachers to examine their thinking and practice critically, often through the active examination of their own school's work.
- The encouragement of study and research, amongst practising teachers, together with the growth of our own interests; the publication of accounts of this work in readable forms.
- The development and evaluation of small-scale innovations amongst committed teachers.

THE NOTTINGHAM STYLE

Perhaps it is not surprising that, during the course of our work with teachers and parents, we have developed a characteristic and distinctive 'Nottingham style', which is based upon a number of views not only about the field of home/school relations, but also about the most effective ways of working and bringing about improvements in practice. Here are some of the key values:

(1) Thinking and practice need to develop together — neither can develop in a healthy, long-term way without the other. This precludes, on the one hand, the uncritical introduction of gimmicky

practices and, on the other, deep philosophical agonising which ignores the need to identify effective forms of action.

(2) Any group of teachers and parents needs to proceed on the assumption of a wide range of attitudes and experience, as this is characteristic of most situations. Developments which are little more than preaching to the converted, or which assume much shared belief and common experience, sooner or later come unstuck as important differences reveal themselves. Besides, significant differences of attitude and behaviour are legitimate and can often be used constructively to challenge views and identify alternative courses of action. In the end you can only build on where you are, not where someone thinks you *ought* to be.

(3) The view of home/school relations embodied in our work is not of a cosy, idealised world where everything in the garden is lovely. Whilst there are currently many interesting challenges and opportunities, there are also many actual and potential pitfalls and obstacles to progress. It doesn't do anybody any good to sweep these under the carpet.

(4) Over the years we have come to reject the narrow sectarian divisions that characterise much INSET work. In particular, we feel that people working in the pre-school, primary, secondary and special education sectors have much to give, and learn from, each other. This is not, of course, a stubborn refusal to acknowledge the special circumstances and features that are peculiar to each, but a belief, based on experience, that the joint exploration of common ground is important and has much to offer.

(5) In educational innovation and development too much attention is frequently given to a 'transplant model' of change. In this approach an attempt is made to graft new approaches on to the existing body of beliefs and practices. Not surprisingly it has a high rate of rejection and failure.

As a response to this experience, we have found it extremely valuable to encourage people to begin with a critical and thorough examination of their *existing* practice, and the assumptions on which it is based, as the crucial first stage in its overhaul and improvement.

(6) Above all, our hallmark has been a growing concern to find practical ways of 'listening to parents', to acknowledge and become more responsive to parental views and experience — the things parents know and are good at — and to act on the basis of what can be learned from this.

Perhaps the best way of portraying the process, which is the basis of the present account, is to follow through a simple example which illustrates 'listening to parents' as a philosophy and a way of working. To do this we have used a 'grounded approach' to the study of parental perspectives and experiences. Rather than start with a theory of how the world is, then try to find some evidence that fits, we have chosen to examine bits of the real world, *then* tried to make sense of them.

The following example shows how the process of listening to parents can identify, from expressions of parental experience and concern, areas for growth and development.

Data

> *Mother (Familiar Parent)*. If they have a parents' evening, like, you know, I go along then. But I prefer the one where you go along and see the kids' work and they come with you, sort of thing, you know.
> *Interviewer*. Oh yes, what, you take the children?
> *Mother*. Yes, and then they show me their work and they explain it. Instead of going up to the teacher and waiting for him to explain it, I look at the kids' books and then they say what they're doing like.

Interpretation

Our samples contained many examples of parents who focused their attempts to understand what the school was doing directly *on their children*, albeit in very different ways . . .

A small but significant number of parents, however, described understandings that had emerged from *the process of asking children to explain their work to them*.

Teacher action

To experiment with a session based upon:

— an aspect of the consultation process that *directly* involves pupils;
— the possibility of links between the formal consultation process and the life and work of the classroom generally;
— the setting of starting-points, targets, etc., which parents and children can follow up, both together and separately;
— an emphasis on process and method (rather than products, marks, grades, etc., which is what parents normally are given).

So 'listening to parents', which is the main theme of this book, needs to be seen as a crucial element in any attempt to improve home/school relations. It is, for us, a key strategy in the identification of parental perspectives and experience, both in general terms and with regard to special needs and particular circumstances. It provides a major focus in the planning and evaluation of home/school activity and professional development in this area. It can make schools aware of the families of their pupils and of the communities in which they are located, more sensitive to the need to consult and share and, possibly, more likely to seek parental co-operation, participation and involvement. Most of all, however, 'listening to parents' is a process that can, in itself, identify important educational knowledge and other resources, areas of actual and potential support, and suggest practical developments and new ways of working.

Part Two

Listening to Parents: Their Perspectives and Experience

4

The Making of Home/School Relations

The growth of interest and activity in the home/school field has already been outlined, and in this chapter what has been described as the 'parent-centred' philosophy is applied to the point where parent and teacher meet for the first time, where the child enters the schooling system for the first time, and where the process of the making of home/school relations can be said to begin. 'Process' implies an element of continuity and development, and it is true to say that the features which characterise this crucial point of entry are built upon and brought sharply into focus from time to time throughout the child's school career. A growing understanding of this process, therefore, and an awareness of its constraints and flexibilities in operation will hopefully assist those interested in effecting positive changes in their own situation.

The over-arching influences of the participants in home/school relations, as they meet to share the education of the child, are represented in Figure 4.1. Relationships of any kind consist of two elements: what the two parties bring to them, and what they then do with what they've brought — a historical or 'biographical' element, and a 'dynamic' element. The biographical element will be made up of past experiences and the way these have shaped their view of themselves and each other, a personal 'philosophy' on the task in which they are engaged, and the knowledge they have of the particular context in which the encounter is to take place. This context includes not only the localised geographical environment, the organisation of the school and its community, but also the wider influence of the ways in which class, culture, race and gender are structured, and how they operate in our society. When it comes to developing strategies for effective home/school relations, an inner-city school with a large proportion of pupils and parents from an

Figure 4.1: The making of home/school relations

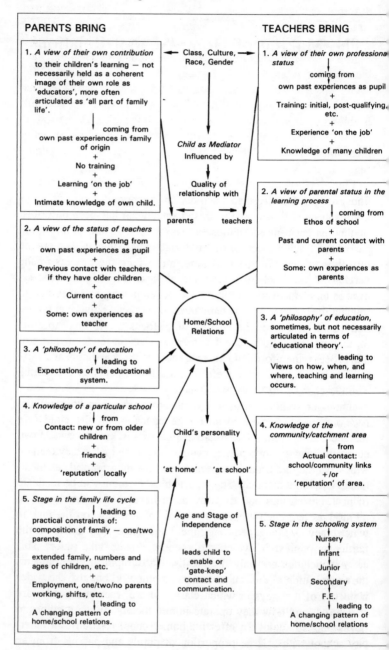

ethnic minority group, for instance, may need to be aware of different elements in the relationship, and to choose different strategies, from a rural school with an homogeneous population.

The 'dynamic' element of home/school relations is represented in Figure 4.1 by reference to its developmental nature. The family and the school move and change through time: they each have a 'life-cycle' and the point in this cycle at which each participant has arrived, will influence what each is looking for, expecting from, and is able to contribute to the relationship with the other. The pupil, of course, is not a passive participant in all this, but rather an active mediator of the relationship, and therefore appears as a central figure in the chart.

Figure 4.1 is intended as an aid to examining particular situations, an analytic 'tool' to be applied wherever and in so far as it illuminates the design, engineering and operation of a particular 'model' of home/school relationships.

We shall now look in some detail at this biographical aspect, and turn then to illustrating the dynamic working-out of the process at various points when teachers and parents meet, before finally examining the making of home/school relations at the point of transfer from nursery to infant school.

THE 'BIOGRAPHY' OF HOME/SCHOOL RELATIONS

This 'biography' is analysed by taking teachers and parents as an example of a professional/lay relationship. In this context, they each have a view of their role, and a view of the other's. In Chapter 7 we shall be looking at what parents actually do in their role as educators, but here the concern is with how *they* see what they do, which is quite different: they hold a view of their own contribution to their children's learning not as a coherent image of themselves as 'educators' but more as participants in 'family life', during which all kinds of learning may take place. The shape of their contribution to such family life stems from their own past experiences in the family in which they grew up, plus plenty of 'learning on the job'. They have had no formal training for this role, but develop as they go along, by trial and error, an intimate knowledge of their own children.

Teachers, on the other hand, have a view of themselves as 'professionals' and this view will have elements rooted in their own past experiences, this time as pupils. In addition, they have undergone formal professional training, initial and perhaps post-qualifying, which is then reinforced and modified by experience 'on the job'. This will lead them to a knowledge of many different children.

As well as a view of themselves, teachers and parents will meet holding a view of the other participant in the relationship. Parents' views of the status of teachers will come from their own past experiences as a pupil (and all involved in education have very powerful memories of these — perhaps that is why, sometimes perversely, we are in education!). Added to these memories, there may be new contacts with teachers, as the parents of older children who have already been through the system, modified by any preliminary contact or communication over the particular child in question. Some parents will also have experience as adults of positions which have familiarised them more intimately with teachers — either as teachers themselves or as school caretakers, dinner-ladies, librarians, school governors, etc.

The teacher's view of parental status in the learning process will be influenced by past and current contact with parents, overlaid by the dominant ethos of the school they are in at the time. Many will also be parents themselves, and this may or may not influence how they see the parents of the children they teach. We have had graphic illustrations from talking to teachers of how such experience as parents may be carried over into a teacher's professional life, ('I found it very difficult to suddenly holler at children any more . . . I know what the difficulties of parents are, and what their anxieties are really . . .'), but they can also be held intact without altering a separately held view of 'parents in general'.

Both participants will also bring a broad 'philosophy' of education to their relationship. For parents, this will lead to certain expectations of the educational system, and these expectations are one of the tools with which they judge a particular institution or teacher. For teachers, such a philosophy will lead to views on how, when, and where teaching and learning occur. Teachers often find it quite difficult to articulate such a philosophy in terms of 'educational theory', and will often use 'rule of thumb' descriptions not too dissimilar in kind to those used by parents. Attempts at defining 'reading readiness' for example, may well lead teachers to offer descriptions of children which sound very similar to parents talking.

Home/school relations, like others, do not take place in a vacuum, and the context in which teachers and parents meet is another element in their biographical luggage. Parents will have some knowledge of the school their child is about to enter, either from older children who have been pupils, or from parents of other children who attend the school, and from the school's reputation locally. Reputations do not necessarily have a one-to-one correspondence with the objects to which they apply and can be the source of great irritation and frustration, as well as of great influence. The same kinds of influence operate on the teacher's knowledge of the community/catchment area of their school. It may be based on real contact, on well-developed school/community links, or largely on the 'reputation' of the area and the kinds of parents who inhabit it.

THE DYNAMICS OF HOME/SCHOOL RELATIONS

As outlined earlier, the participants will be at a particular *stage* in their biographies. The family life-cycle will impose constraints of size and composition: one/two parents, grandparents, 'extended' family, the ages of the children, etc. And once again, it will be subject to structural influences such as the institutional aspects of race in our society, the incidence of poverty and wealth, health and illness, employment and the forms it takes — one/two/no parents working, shiftwork, etc.

Teachers, likewise, will be subject to the constraints imposed by the particular stage of the schooling system in which they teach: from nursery through to FE and the interaction of the two parties at particular stages in the 'life-cycle' of their respective institutions will lead to a *changing* pattern of home/school relations.

Finally, this changing pattern is mediated by the pupils themselves, who exert an influence according to: the quality of their relationship with their parents, the quality of their relationship with their teachers, their own personality (perhaps this should be plural, as we so often hear descriptions of two — an 'at home' personality and an 'at school' personality), and the age and stage of independence at which the child has arrived, or is determined to work towards! These factors will lead them, in varying degrees, to 'enable' or to 'gate-keep' contact and communication between parents and teachers.

Parents anticipate their children's entry into the schooling system with ambivalent feelings, composed of a mixture of excitement, relief, anxiety and loss. Many teachers would agree that they also approach the beginning of term and the arrival of a new group of children with ambivalent feelings, if for different reasons. So what happens when the two meet to share the education of their children, in what has become known, if not carefully scrutinised, as an educational 'partnership'?

As any parent will know, it is a big step to hand over your child's care and development to someone else, and in the case of schooling, it is because teachers are seen as professionals that this sharing of one's children is seen as appropriate. But the ambivalence of parents mentioned earlier also stems from the fact that teachers are professionals, because this makes them very powerful figures indeed. This assertion may raise a wry smile or worse from teachers who have recently been engaged in a demoralising conflict with the government, but it is a revealing exercise to bring an interdisciplinary perspective to bear, and to compare the lay parents' approach to their child's teacher with the mixture of feelings invoked by a visit to the doctor, to the solicitor, or a visit from the health visitor. It is an asymmetrical relationship, and the 'professionalism' of the one may be as significant in accounting for this as the other more commonly noted factors such as social class. 'Consumers' who may see themselves or be seen as having equal, or even higher, status in their own field than the professionals they are approaching, are still aware of this, because the professional is seen to possess the kind of expert knowledge that they themselves do not have. This can even be the case with parents who are teachers, when they visit their own children's teachers at a consultation evening, and it may go some way towards explaining why, in the past, professional perspectives have dominated relations between home and school, and why they have been viewed primarily through the eyes of schools and teachers, and on their terms.

We are attempting to incorporate into home/school relations a parental perspective which acknowledges that for any given situation, issue, communication, or interaction between teachers and parents, there will be more than one way of defining what the contact is about. The teacher's and the parent's definition of the task may coincide or it may conflict.

We have already seen how the two parties bring different biographical elements to the relationship and, at any given time, these may be operating via different viewpoints, purposes and strategies to facilitate or obstruct effective home/school relations. It is how these potentially differing perspectives operate in practice, in the day-to-day contacts between parents and teachers, which constitutes the 'making of home/school relations'. How this 'dynamic' aspect of the relationship works can now be examined in a number of settings where teachers and parents meet to share the educational task.

A CURRICULUM WORKSHOP

Until recently, the curriculum was seen to be the exclusive territory of schools and teachers. Parents would feel very tentative indeed about making claims about what was taught and how this was to be done. All that has changed: it may seem sometimes that everyone has a right to tell teachers how to do their job! In fact, claims on the curriculum that have always been there are now being made more explicit, and vociferous parents, the local community, the government, pressure groups, trade unions, industry and employers are all now making their voices heard. What seemed to be 'taken for granted' in the past is at the centre of noisy and painful debate — the context, content, and form of sex education being a recent example of this.

What happens when schools try to communicate with parents about the curriculum? It is suggested that in this area, as in the areas of parent/teacher consultation and advice given to parents about helping their children at home, teacher-perspectives dominate parent-perspectives in practice, by more attention being given to the form of the contact than to its purpose. The purpose of contacts, from an event such as a curriculum workshop to a small-scale piece of interaction like a two-minute conversation as a mother delivers her child to nursery, is often not part of the teacher's agenda. Much valuable effort and imagination can be wasted because there has been a 'presentation' to an 'audience', which has failed to take into account why the audience has come, and what they are looking and listening *for*.

At a local infants' school, teachers put a lot of effort into the organisation of a curriculum workshop. A successful written invitation had produced 26 women and 8 men, there was a welcome from the Head, with coffee served to parents by the staff, and then the parents broke into groups to try out three different kinds of mathematical equipment in turn, under teacher guidance, before meeting back in the Hall for a plenary session of questions and answers. Different games were explained, demonstrated, and played in the groups, with cuisenaire rods, logiblocks and sets. The atmosphere was relaxed and informal, and the proceedings were

29

lubricated with good humour.

Parent groups were kept moving round the tasks by the bell ringing, and the schedule was successfully completed. Not many questions were asked at the end, but parents said they had really asked their questions going round in the groups. The impression of the participant observer at this event was one of a warm staff and enthusiastic parents, who may not have fully understood the use of the equipment but who on the whole felt reassured and satisfied that a good job was being done with their children. One particular parent, however, had asked some very challenging questions about the lack of proper sums in the books her son brought home. She had been used to seeing pages of figures, (e.g. $4 + 3 = 7$) in her older children's books and could not see the connection between the equipment she'd seen, the talk she'd heard of 'factors', 'attributes' and 'developing logical thinking' and the written sums she recognised and which her older children had readily mastered. The reassurances which one or two other 'supportive' parents were anxious to give, along the lines of children *understanding* what the sum *means* as opposed to simply performing the operation, did not convince her.

How successful can this event be seen to be? And what did it contribute to home/school relations? To answer that requires us to ask questions about its purpose. If it was an attempt to explain experiential methods of learning mathematical concepts, it probably attempted far too much in a short space of time. Parents probably felt personally disabled and convinced that 'number work' definitely needed to be left to teachers. If it was a 'PR' exercise to demonstrate to parents that teachers know what they are doing, are well organised, and that learning can be fun, it seemed to be very successful. In terms of home/school relations, the implicit message may have been that this area of the curriculum can safely be left to teachers. If it was an attempt to incorporate the kinds of understanding of, and familiarity with maths that parents possess, with the routes to mathematical competence used in the school, it must be said to have failed with at least one parent — the kind of parent very familiar to most teachers. She may not be convinced, whatever approach is taken. Perhaps there is a group of parents which is simply looking for operational competence without understanding because this is what they see their child as able to achieve, or because in their experience this is all adult life requires. How valid a viewpoint is this? Teachers may continue to have other aims, but it is the fact that such divergence is not explicitly acknowledged or taken aboard that is significant in the making of home/school relations. The continuing debate being conducted on the curriculum is due to its value-laden nature, illustrated but not on the agenda of this curriculum workshop for parents. It is worth listening to parents before discussing the purposes, and planning the organisation, of such curriculum events.

PARENTS' EVENINGS

The same is true for teacher/parent consultation evenings. The purposes of such encounters are discussed in detail later in the book when considering the development of effective practice, but what form such contact takes is once again significant for home/school relations. With consultation evenings, that form is very often problem-centred, both teachers and parents often commenting that where all is going well there is 'not much point' to the meeting. Problems constitute a threat to the teacher's professional status and a number of strategies, from denial to prevarication, reassurance, or more rarely, concrete advice, may be used in order to resolve the problem and 'manage' the parent, whilst protecting the teacher's own professional identity. The negotiation which takes place in handling problems is another element in the making of home/school relations, and the mapping out of the parts to be played by teachers and parents respectively can be illustrated by several examples.

This mother explains how she noticed her son's poor spelling when examining his work at his junior school parents' evening, and attempted for the first time to intervene:

We looked in his books . . . you could read what he'd written, but the way he'd spelled things! — and we drew these teachers' attention to it at the time, and they sort of poo-poo-ed us, made us feel a bit silly, 'Oh, we don't put any importance on spelling. He's got a very good vocabulary. Provided we can understand what he's trying to say, that will do.' We brought it up again when he started at the Comprehensive school, because he was getting no better, and I suggested that we did a spelling list: 'Oh, no, don't pressure him, leave it', 'let us do the teaching, you do the parenting' sort of thing; . . . and with the result that Andrew is 17 and still his spelling is really poor . . . we felt a bit, erm, metaphorically as though we'd had our hands smacked for even suggesting . . .

Feeling thoroughly frustrated and impotent, and sensitive to the label she might have acquired from the school — 'I think I got where they p'raps thought I was getting a bit neurotic about it' — she did not bring the subject up again until Andrew was about to take his exams. She seems to see it as significant that at this point she had become social equals with Andrew's teacher, and that this enabled the teacher to be honest with her about Andrew's abilities:

Then we went to the parents' evening prior to Andrew taking his exams. We went to this English teacher, who incidentally before she started to take Andrew . . . we became friends. They took the kids on a skiing holiday with the school, and we got to know her on a sort of social . . . yeah . . . and they used to visit, and when we went to see her, I said, 'What d'you think Ellen? What're his chances?' Well you can't imagine how I felt when she turned round and said, 'Well, I've never seen spelling like it. He doesn't really stand a chance.' I turned to her then, and I said, 'I could scream.' All these years we've said, 'Please, what can we do?' and there they were saying 'No, don't push him', and then we've got one honest person who turned round and said . . . and I tell you, most of the time, we were laughed at . . . in fact, at one parents' evening I went, I said 'Well, how do you expect to become successful if you can't spell?' and he said, 'If Andrew's successful, he'll have a secretary who can spell', which I thought was a bit flippant.

Prevarication, reassurance and dismissal were strategies used to 'manage' this parent's problem:

Mother. I think he's a little bit less concentrating than all the other children . . . and I mentioned this . . . I said, 'My little boy doesn't seem to be able to concentrate for two seconds on something' . . . and the headmistress said, 'Oh, all children are like that!' so I thought, 'Oh, thank goodness! He's no different to any other!' but, er, his teacher said that he did seem to concentrate just a little bit less than all the others.
Interviewer. Did she give you any suggestions?
Mother, Well, I asked her. I said, 'Well, what can we do?' and she said, 'Well, do nothing at the moment. He might just, sort of, come out of it. It just might be that he's a, going to be a late developer, and just come out of it of his own accord.'

The mother herself had observed her son's lack of concentration. This was brought up independently to her by the class teacher. She sought advice at an Open Evening but had her fears dismissed by the Head. This did not allay them, however, and her suspicions were again confirmed by the class teacher. She was unable to follow the only advice she received, which was to 'do nothing but wait and see' and she went on to attempt to 'instil in him that he's got to learn how to sit still' and submit to 'being taught'.

A term later, this child was described by the infant teacher as follows:

> a very *lively* boy (*meaningful look*). He can cause a bit of uproar in the classroom, yes, he needs to be sat on (*laughs*) and er, he's an immature little boy you know, he's still very much got many baby ways, lots yes. He's very, a clumsy little boy, his motor control is really very poor. He falls over his own feet and this kind of thing, you know. He's er, he's a stiff little boy when it comes to moving.

This emerging identity had not been communicated to the parent, who recounted that he was settling down satisfactorily in the infant school. Whether she had come to accept the school's earlier reassurances or whether she had decided to 'leave it to the professionals' was not clear.

Other parents who perceive a 'problem' are more successful in negotiating an outcome whereby their definition of the situation prevails, and without the teacher feeling that he has to 'manage' the parent. The following example is one where the teacher did not feel his own professional identity was being threatened by the parent's suggestion, and where both felt that they had together achieved a satisfactory result for the child:

> He used to moan like buggery about this French, and we went down to school . . . and we had a word with his French teacher, and we put it to him, that in our opinion he wasn't being given enough incentive, a big enough carrot, and the French teacher said that in a while, they were going to be segregated, and those that were catching on very quickly would be put together — and this worked. We haven't had any moans out of him, have we? Because every time he goes, he's given something to do, a target to aim for, and he'll go for it.

Parents like this father sometimes choose their tactics when preparing for a parents' evening, aware of the need for sensitive negotiation:

> As I say, if we go down and put the case as . . . genuinely interested parents . . . and not er, the type of parent who will immediately go down to school because his son's been told off, and you know, the teacher can't do that.

These phrases 'put the case' and 'genuinely interested parents' which he used frequently, highlight the element of negotiation which is integral to the parent/teacher consultation interview, and form the nuts and bolts of the making of home/school relations.

STARTING SCHOOL AS THE MAKING OF HOME/SCHOOL RELATIONS

Up until children enter formal schooling, the parents have had primary responsibility for their learning. The point of a child's first entry into school, therefore, provides valuable insight into the making of home/school relations and into how teachers and parents are assigned particular roles in the child's learning. It is at this point also that parents are perhaps most keen to seek advice about how they can help their children at home.

As already touched upon, parents do not have a well-defined picture of themselves as 'educators' and are largely unconscious of the skills and expertise they possess in this area. It is perhaps this fact which predisposes them to be even more receptive to what the professional has to say about how, when, and where, children learn. As to the 'where', parents are very conscious, at this point, of the school as an institution, and the learning that takes place there is seen as 'proper' learning. For parents at the infant school mentioned earlier, nursery was seen as a transitional stage *en route* to school. Although all the parents viewed it very positively, its benefits were seen as largely *social* in nature, a preparation for the infant school rather than as an educational experience in its own right — 'He's been to nursery, and they've sort of, knocked him into shape a bit', as one father put it. Parents were familiar with the concept of 'learning through play' but *what* was learned was rarely articulated, and the nursery curriculum was contrasted with the 'proper' learning that would take place in the infant school. In describing the difference between the two curricula, parents contrasted play with work. Proper learning denoted the accomplishment of the skills of reading and writing, and for this to be achieved, the requirements frequently repeated by parents were those of sitting down and concentration. The phrase 'sitting and learning' was common: the two were seen as going together.

We are not suggesting that this perception is inaccurate, and that learning to write, for example, can be achieved without sitting down! What is significant, however, is that a sharp distinction was becoming apparent between the *kinds* of learning which take place in the nursery and the infant school, and between the *ways* in which children learn in the two places. What is being learned in a particular setting may not be clearly understood, as with another group of mothers who after watching their children through a school window using Dienes attribute blocks, recounted to us with some disgust that their children were too old to be playing with bricks!

The parents at the nursery did not associate nursery play with *cognitive* as opposed to social learning. The fact that many nursery teachers' colleagues in primary and secondary schools may share this perception does not detract from the undervaluing of the nursery curriculum and the kinds of learning which take place there, which this represents.

Proper, cognitive learning appeared to be reserved for the infant school: 'the rest of the time [at nursery] they just play, where at school, they learn more than . . . you know, the play *is* learning, they play to learn, but when they go to school, they really . . .', one mother tried to explain. And this kind of learning requires sitting down, concentrating, and a loss of freedom to pursue an activity for as long or short a time as one wishes — 'at the moment she thinks that you can sort of get up and have a little skip and then come back to it, you know' — not because you can't control a pencil when you're moving around, but because of an additional element in the learning process: being taught. The initiative for learning shifts, with the child's move from the nursery to the infant school, from herself to the teacher:

I'd say, 'Well, it's going to be *different* when you go into [the infant] class. You've got to sit down, and she's going to actually *teach* you how to read, and how to write', and I said, 'You've got to sit still while she actually teaches you all this.'

The results produced by these changes sometimes seem

miraculous to the parent. Parents who had tried unsuccessfully to introduce their son to the sitting and learning routine before he actually started at the infant school, were most impressed not only by how quickly he had adapted to the constraints of school, but by the fact that he had learned to write his name as a result:

> Before he started school, he didn't know how to write his name. We'd sit with him and say, 'Come on, let's see if we can learn you how to write your name', and he just wasn't bothered about sitting down learning . . . but he hadn't been at that school a fortnight, and he was coming home, and he's wrote his name. It was in a fashion, but you know, he'd write his name, and that I think really surprised us. He came home, he says, 'Look, I've wrote me name!' It were all up and down, but he'd wrote it, you know, and I thought, 'Crike! In a couple of weeks! He's done it already!'

The formula for this play/work dichotomy seems to be something like this: the nursery curriculum consists of play which leads to social learning. This has the comparatively low status of merely being a preparation, although it is pleasant and allows considerable freedom on the part of the child. The role of the teacher as educator is peripheral. The curriculum of the infant school consists of work, which leads to academic learning with recognisable products. It is of higher status, and there is an element of the protestant work ethic — an acceptance that you may not like it, but it will be good for you. The unpleasantness may come from the greater degree of compulsion or direction, and the intervention of the teacher in the learning process is central.

It seems, too, that parents do not make a clear distinction between what might be described as the academic content of the curriculum and that part of it via which the child is socialised into the institution of the school and learns to become a pupil. For the parents at this school, the two were synonymous, or it seemed at least that one could not occur without the other: learning to be a pupil was seen to be a prerequisite of learning how to read or write. It certainly seemed to be so in practice for the young son of the parents previously quoted. The failure, however, to make a distinction between learning and institutional socialisation has important implications for the roles of parents and teachers as educators, and for the relationship between them. We may ask for whose benefit, and to what purpose, do these parents attempt to prepare their children for the rigorous life of the infant classroom. Is it so that they will be better equipped for the learning process, or so that they will 'slot in and tick away nicely' as one mother expressed it, without incurring the teacher's wrath or making her job more difficult? The two may be the same in practice, but when parents fail to recognise the institutional component of learning at school — and it is surely this to which all the talk of 'sitting and learning' and 'concentration' refers — they accord the person of the teacher more credit than she is due, and devalue accordingly their own potential contribution. It results in the kind of admiration for teachers which Elizabeth and John Newson describe in their lively and fascinating book, *Perspectives on school at seven years old* (Allen and Unwin, London, 1977):

> Many parents express deep admiration for the way teachers surmount what appears to be the almost impossible task of controlling such an enormous 'family', and it is clear that their admiration stems from this false comparison with their own parental role. Surely teachers must be super-human if they can deal with thirty children single-handed! Imagine what it would be like if their own families were to be increased by a factor of ten! It is this mixture of awe and sympathy which can lead parents to ignore their children's complaints, feeling that they themselves could not do such a job and therefore have no right to criticise if something goes wrong.

And it was the above parents' failure to recognise what the Newsons call the 'powerful and convincing reasons' of the school organisational machine that led to their admiration of the school for teaching their son to write his name in two weeks, when they themselves had failed even to get him to sit down with a pencil.

THE TEACHER'S CONTRIBUTION

How far do teachers contribute to this picture of themselves as able to achieve the kinds of results that parents apparently cannot? The most striking message parents received at this school about the learning that goes on in school is that there is a right and a wrong way of going about it. Implicit in this idea is the notion that the school knows and is competent in the right way, and that parents use the wrong way, with potentially disastrous consequences for the child:

> I would like to know the proper ways to go about it, you know.

I went wrong about it with the alphabet, so I mean, I could spoil it for her, going to school. I could've learnt her all back to front, and it's going to take them a lot longer to get the right way . . . we can do more harm than good, can't we, if we don't know what we're doing.

The same message had apparently been communicated at a school meeting attended by these parents:

They shown us the way *they* learn 'em, 'cos I can understand their point of view when you teach 'em *your* way, and then they've got to teach 'em the *right* way, sort of, you know.

For the following parent, the dangers had been made quite explicit, and to avoid the risk of confusing the child, the parent should apparently refrain from doing anything and leave the job to the professionals right from the beginning:

But his teacher said she prefers them to come to school not knowing nothing, she says, because sometimes parents are showing them one way, and it's different to *our* way, and the children are getting confused, thinking, well, me mum showed me how to do it this way, and me teacher's shown me how to do it this, you know, so she says, I prefer children to come like your Stephen, not knowing nothing — and then she can sort of show 'em right from scratch, you know, right from the beginning . . . and when we think about it, it is the best way.

Other parents, receiving the same message from this school, and having thought about it, did not think it the best way, and refused to be ascribed such a limited role:

I did once ask if there was any way I could do anything for Jenny at home . . . they found it better if we just left it to them. We weren't . . . I don't think really they like you to do anything with them at all . . . they like you to be involved in the things they do at school, but as far as your child's work and things like that are concerned, I think they like you to leave that to them. They like you to join in with anything that's going off at school — sport and all that — you're involved in all that, but the actual work that the child does, I think they just prefer to tell you their bit.

This mother nevertheless continued to do what she felt to be 'her bit': 'I *try* to teach her myself, I'm not bothered what they think, to be honest!' This mother had only gone out to try to teach her daughter herself after having been given a message of exclusion — 'they found it better if we just left it to them'. Most parents *are* bothered about what 'they' think, and whilst being very keen to help their children in whatever way they can, usually ask teachers for guidance before proceeding. We have heard from several parents what form that guidance took. Did the reception teacher confirm this? She did confirm the parents' concern with enabling their child to 'slot in' satisfactorily to the school institution:

> *Interviewer.* What sort of questions do they ask, what do they seem concerned about?
> *Teacher.* Well, strangely enough (*laughs*) a lot of the questions are more, kind of 'Do they need a pair of plimsolls?' you know (*laughs*), not very many deep questions about the work, you know.

The one thing the parents all wanted to know regarding learning, she went on, was: 'Is there anything I can do to help them to read?' and her response to this, she said, was to tell parents:

> The best thing to do is to read stories to them, *look* at books with them, and talk about them, and play *games* with them, like snap . . . and *matching* things, to do some of the basic skills of beginning to read . . . to talk to them a lot, show interest in what the children want to do, spend time with them . . . answering their questions . . . take them about on Saturdays and show them things . . . extend their vocabulary by taking them about and explaining things to them . . . this is the best thing as far as reading's concerned particularly . . . to give them a broad . . . a . . . you know . . . extend their language.

Why was it that this kind of unimpeachable advice did not seem to be heard by parents? It may be that they were most sensitive to other kinds of message that mixed in. The advice to spend *time* with your children and to take them out on Saturdays is doubtless something that all parents follow, but the demands of family life are many, and what sounds like a need to set special time aside could induce a feeling of guilt (endemic anyway to parenthood) and inadequacy. There is also the question of how necessary it is to see environments for

39

learning in that way, which we will look at later.

In addition, the teacher felt:

> Of course, one of the most important things is not to get, for the parents to get, *tensed up* you know, about their children, because they pass this tension on to them, and particularly if their child shows signs that, they're going to be a *slow reader*, you know, slow learner, then parents are inclined to get a bit uptight if they think that . . . and there's always a danger of passing this tension on to the children.

It is one of a teacher's strengths to have an awareness of the spectrum of 'normal' development, and not to have so much invested in one child that she becomes tensed up about such variation. Every parent, however, wants the best for her/his child. The anxiety that can accompany this is not only entirely understandable, but is also surmountable in ways which do not necessarily exclude parents altogether from the learning process, or consign them to the margins, to helping and supporting teachers, in *their* work:

> They're nice parents, very helpful parents, they're co-operative, you don't get many who will not co-operate with you, I like them myself . . . very ordinary people, but *nice* people, kind people — if you ask for anything in the school, they're only too eager to help.

The parents at this school *were* only too eager to help and spoke in their turn very positively of the school, the teachers, its openness to parents, its parents' rooms, its parents' evenings, etc., and by and large they accepted the supporting role they were assigned in the process of the making of home/school relations. They accepted that the school knew the right way of doing things, and that their intervention could damage this essentially professional activity. Some were happy enough to 'leave it to them', and impressed by the results the teachers produced, but those who did have anxieties did not have them allayed by prevarication. Almost as a self-fulfilling prophecy, we saw the mother impress on her son, in a way that indeed sounded tensed up and uptight, that he'd got to 'sit still and be taught'.

TOWARDS A RE-DEFINITION . . . !

That dimension of the making of home/school relations which involves the professionalisation of learning, therefore, can, at the same time, assign parents to the margins of the learning process, and take initiative away from the child, who becomes a passive recipient: 'His teacher said she prefers them to come to school not knowing nothing . . . and then she can sort of show 'em right from scratch.' There are alternative models of professionalism for teachers, which also accommodate alternative models for parents as educators.

Because of the social and economic changes in society touched upon earlier, with many forms and patterns of family living now in existence, the role of the professional is a very complex one. It involves a recognition of a pluralistic society in which different values co-exist. Such a recognition is especially difficult to put into practice, but especially important for the educationalist, who is involved in the transmission of culture. The questions arise, 'Which culture?', 'Whose culture?' And there is, of course, no single solution or response. It is in this context that the approach of 'listening to parents' is so relevant. And it is not only relevant but effective, in that, for those who are interested in examining the making of home/school relations in their own settings, and in improving their own practice, it is an approach which *works*, as it expands the possibilities for real contact and opens up new ground. It offers new explanations for old phenomena, and treats people as individuals rather than excluding whole 'groups'.

Parents are not unaware of the mythology surrounding the 'parents-who-never-come' theme. A parent who is very involved in his son's comprehensive school illustrated how he had absorbed some of this professional ideology when he commented recently that '70 per cent of parents aren't interested.' Many other parents become alienated by such assumptions. Listening to parents quickly counters these, and begins to throw up other kinds of explanation for what has been interpreted as lack of interest.

For those who do not see education as a route to mobility for 'people like them', for those who are unfamiliar with the rules of the game or who encounter the system at its most intransigent points, or those who are keen to help but are unaware of their own skills and potential and therefore ready to accept a supporting role, the judgemental approach which assumes a monopoly of knowledge and expertise is simply counter-productive — it does not 'work', whichever way you look at it. The phrase 'the right way' not only fails to exploit what parents can offer, but implies a consensus within the profession itself which does not in fact exist.

Teachers, and particularly those who have the opportunity for informal contact with parents of young children, may say, 'But we do listen to parents, every day when they bring their children to school we have a chat.' In the context of the making of home/school relations, however, 'listening' is a much more systematic affair, and we would not wish to underestimate the amount of effort it requires — it is an active approach, not a passive stance. Initially it involves an act of faith in suspending any assumptions about 'parental interest'. Or even going so far as reversing the estimation quoted above, and assuming that it is a tiny minority of parents who are genuinely not interested in their children's learning, or at least not in the kinds of learning on offer in schools, and searching for alternative explanations for those whose positions and perceptions are not yet recognisable.

It then becomes part of the professional teacher's role to discover kinds of learning other than the already familiar school-based kinds, and to enable parents to discover and develop the contribution they make to this process. If asked directly what educative roles they play towards their child, many parents will say that they don't! Encouraged further, they can go on to describe practices and approaches that many teachers would admire and applaud. Parents do not know what they know! For teachers who wish to work towards a more genuine partnership in home/school relations, listening to parents can be the beginning of creating different but complementary roles for the professional teacher and the lay parent.

5

The Development of Familiarity and Understanding

In the previous chapter, considerable emphasis was given to the ways in which home/school relationships are 'made'. This was done through an examination of some of the ways in which the foundations are laid in the initial stages of a child's school career and of some of the ways in which parental expectations are met and modified. The future development of these relationships is shown as being heavily dependent upon rather one-sided models of contact and negotiation.

Whilst continuing to share some of these developing concerns, the present chapter deliberately changes the focus of its attention. For in this chapter the spotlight falls mainly upon parents who, for a number of different reasons and in a variety of ways, have chosen to have more active and involved relationships with their children's formal education. Their children also happen to attend schools which openly profess a commitment to, and active support for, a fuller partnership with the parents of their pupils, and have something of a reputation for the quality of the arrangements they make to bring this about.

So the emphasis has switched to parents with considerable experience of dealing with their children's schools. Sometimes this derives from having a large family, or from frequent changes of school or location, as happens with service families or those of young executives; others get to know schools better than most parents because of their voluntary involvement, helping around the school, joining a Mums' Group or the PTA or becoming an elected parent governor. A small but significant minority have had the opportunity of seeing the life and work of the school from behind the scenes, through a variety of part-time ancillary jobs as dinner-ladies, welfare assistants and school secretaries. In many cases, such mothers had been recruited from the ranks of parents who had previously served their apprenticeship in a voluntary capacity, before becoming suitable cases for adoption. So, in one way or another, these parents embody a great deal of experience, based on their very varied dealings with their children's schools.

Such a cross-section provides an excellent opportunity to see how far the rhetoric of partnership is being translated into effective action and to examine some of the consequences of opening up schools to parents in what appears, on the surface, to be favourable circumstances. The study of such a sample also sought a clearer picture of some of the consequences of increased contact and involvement. In particular, we were interested in finding out whether increasing familiarity led to:

a greater willingness to intervene on a child's behalf;
a greater confidence in tackling school-related activities at home;
a wider commitment to the life and work of the school;
a deeper interest in the processes of education themselves.

In spite of these questions in our minds, however, we considered that these parents should not be regarded as a different species. For whilst they *do* often have access to information and opportunities to see and discuss aspects of their children's schooling, much of their contact runs parallel to that of 'ordinary' parents, only in a more heightened form.

In a similar way, an examination of the experience of familiar parents (not only here but throughout our work) attempts to bring together a view of the everyday assumptions which parents make and sustain and those special occasions when these can be challenged or threatened. The everyday view gives emphasis to the role of pupils as mediators between home and school, and to the normal arrangements that most schools make for regular and continuing communication and contact; an interest in special occasions draws attention to particular circumstances and critical incidents in parents' dealings with schools and teachers. The practical implications of this distinction are more fully explored in Part Three.

So we have divided our attention between the normal, the predictable, the commonplace and particular moments of insight and understanding, attempting to assess the significance of both for those involved, although it is the latter that is often more noticeable:

Special circumstances/critical incidents: some common examples
- Encounters with particular teachers.
- The experience of visiting school on the spur of the moment.
- The arrival of an unexpectedly bad report.
- The revelation of important differences between children within the family that can't be readily explained.
- Encounters with new subjects, teaching methods or school policies.

Finally, before moving on to listen to the voices of a particular collection of parents, it is necessary to say that we have attempted to combine distinct traditions of study and investigation in the home/school field, each with its own characteristic concerns, methods of inquiry and approaches to analysis. So we have examined the beliefs and attitudes of parents, attempting to unravel their influence upon, and response to, their behaviour; so, too, we have taken into account a consideration of the structural features of schools and families, such as differences between primary and secondary schools, or changes in the organisation of family life; we have also tried to form a picture of the actual interaction that takes place between schools and families, teachers and parents and explore its significance. It is, however, only when these three lines of enquiry and analysis are combined in a constructive way that a useful framework can emerge with which to examine *parental ideology, opportunity and experience.*

The following pages attempt to sketch, in outline, a picture that uses parental ideology, opportunity and experience as points of reference. It is probably more accurate to liken the picture to a series of snapshots taken from different angles, rather than a single view. For familiarity does not follow a tidy path or logical development; it also contains sharp contrasts, contradictions and paradoxes which together prompt as many questions as solutions.

The account begins with a brief look at two characteristic themes, then shifts to introduce a number of facets of familiarity. Some attempt is then made to draw out some of the wider issues, together with their implications for the development of thinking and practice.

45

'BECOMING FAMILIAR': TWO ILLUSTRATIONS

Parental access and opportunity

The schools which we have studied are not nearly as open to parents as they think they are, or would like to be! For, in spite of parents' apparent familiarity with their children's schools and teachers, access was both conditional and limited. Some areas were freely accessible; others involved negotiated access and conditional entry; finally, there were 'no-go' and taboo areas. These constraints can be illustrated most sharply in relation to access to the staffroom. In one school, access was easy and natural, with particular parents having their own mugs. In another, the staffroom was the impenetrable holy of holies!

There are similar differences with regard to occupied classrooms. Whilst classroom architecture can be seen to be a factor here, a better explanation can be traced through the relationships between the school's philosophy and the pedagogy of individual classrooms. The following extract, drawn from an interview with the head of a very friendly and otherwise 'open' junior school, shows how such a philosophy might be used to legitimate closed classrooms, in ways that contradict the school's expressed and practised home/school policies in other areas.

> I didn't really feel I could dictate to people [staff] that they must do this . . . The difference probably comes when it's a matter of trespassing into a teacher's classroom . . . I have to tread carefully when it comes to a matter of trespassing where they, in the area of the school where there's this immensely strong sense of ownership and belonging, where the teacher runs the room. And it's peculiar to primary schools because this is the room where they are *all* the time, it's their base, where they keep all their personal possessions and it becomes an extension of themselves for the whole year.

So the relationship between 'open schools' and 'closed class-rooms' can often appear to parents to be a contradiction which is hard to understand and difficult to handle. It can also serve to undermine much of the effort a school might make on other fronts.

In providing opportunities for parental access, schools filter and screen opportunities for parents to see the life and work of the school, often in a very limiting way. This is done through a variety of both formal and informal ways, containing both conscious and unrecognised elements. It is, though, accurate to say that these schools underestimate the extent to which this happens and the consequences of it. In addition to the demarcation and defence of territory, parental involvement is also 'managed' through the *screening of people*. Here, the filters operate to let in 'desirable' parents (however these are defined), and to keep others out. Although the criteria for inclusion may be task-related (baking with pupils, costumes for the school play), they more often appear to be person-related, with an emphasis upon intelligence, speech and manner. Whilst parents appear to be generally aware of the different kinds of reason for their inclusion or exclusion, the study contains one very striking example of a mother who very much wants to help in classrooms but feels the school is deliberately keeping her at arm's length, a perception which would shock the headteacher concerned. This process is often reported by parents as being a potential source of bad feeling amongst excluded parents, as well as a differentiating mechanism causing divisions and unrepresentative cliques within the parent body, though it is reported as hearsay rather than being supported by hard evidence.

Such restrictions, then, are achieved through a combination of openly expressed policies and also subtle insinuations, hints and gentle, but perceptible, resistances. Such understandings, in short, are the product of a 'negotiated order', albeit lop-sided, arrived at through the interaction of teachers, pupils and parents.

Another source of differentiated opportunity and access can be traced to the nature of a parent's special interest and involvement. So PTA officials, *in that role*, often experience most of their contact with the school 'after hours', when the classrooms are empty. Their contact will be restricted to a few members of staff connected with the PTA, and often focused upon the school office. Dinner-ladies, by contrast, spend much longer, daily periods within the school, but in a role that is restricted in other ways. Whilst they have plenty of opportunity to observe teacher/pupil interaction in the rather special arena provided by the school meals service, they have little or no contact with classroom life.

In a third example school welfare assistants, like dinner-ladies, have low-status work. Unlike them, however, they have (on the basis of the present sample) extensive opportunities to talk to pupils and to examine their work in the course of patrolling classrooms at lunchtime. The sample contains several striking examples of familiarity with and insight into children's work and the ways it was produced, obtained by talking with children in wet lunchtimes in junior school classrooms!

> I think they've got a *marvellous* set of teachers in this school. I mean, we supervisors, you can go and talk to them, or if we have any trouble with any of them we've only to go and see them and they'll 'elp us. You know, I think they've got a marvellous education here. I mean we get more involved with these children, what we look after at dinner-time. When it's rainin' and we got into the classrooms, when we get more involved with the work they've done. 'Oh, we've done this miss', 'I've done that, miss', you know, it's nice, just seeing, because they tell you about it on the yard, but you're not so involved on the yard as what you are in that classroom (*pause*) . . . I think it's nice. I mean, just before Easter there's a class down 'ere, I think they were third year, they'd made some patterns of, uh, Easter flowers. I've never seen anything so *beautiful*, and they was all along the wall, and they was *marvellous*. But that's credit due to that teacher for showing 'em 'ow to do it.

So these parents, like others, derive their experience from a wider range of opportunities and possibilities. These are shaped both by the philosophy and practice of individual schools, which can vary enormously, and by the special nature of a parent's interest and involvement. However, it is arguable how far it is possible to talk about 'a dinner-lady's view' or a 'PTA view' since these are, of necessity, mediated through educational ideologies which themselves have their roots in social background, status and experience.

Making judgements

These parents put together a picture of their children's progress that, in varying degrees, satisfies their need to be informed and to understand. They do this generally by combining, according to both preference and opportunity, different forms of information and evidence, using one to check out or illuminate another:

> *Interviewer.* Can . . . I ask you how you got a picture of the progress your children were making at this stage?
> *Mother.* I think by a combination of looking at what they were

bringing home and, erm, talking to the teachers and looking at what they had been doing during the term, uh, on the open days.

Father. And seeing what things they did. If they read books at a certain age or, they didn't have to be chivied into reading books. You know, they could clearly add up money.

* * *

Mother. Yes, I do, because all the bookwork that they work with they keep in a box. So if you're early, or even if the teacher's running late you can sit and look through your child's work and take in comments what the teacher's written. So you've got a rough idea how they're going on in maths, English and other subjects by looking at the books, seeing what work they're doing and teachers' comments in them. Whereas, on the senior side, you don't see any of the books, you know you're just reading, they do like a report on ya.

Schools, as the second quotation shows, can choose to communicate about different issues, and in different ways. They also adopt differing and varied kinds of contact and communication and develop different degrees of openness with parents and others. However familiar or experienced parents might be, making a judgement is seldom easy or straightforward. Various messages and experiences have to be checked out. Contradictory accounts have to be set against one another and fresh evidence sought. Conflicting ideas and experience require to be resolved and puzzles unravelled.

The judgement that derives from the combining of information and evidence, itself derives from different modes of perception and experience. Some parents stress the importance, for them, of the authoritative voice of the trained teacher; others emphasise their belief in independent enquiry and the value of judging 'for themselves'. Some parents, sensing a difficulty, patiently monitor the education of their children, building up a detailed dossier before they feel entitled to draw conclusions; for others, such judgements are both immediate and obvious. Then there are the parents for whom judgement comes after a ruminative process in which information and argument are teased out, turned over reflectively and patiently evaluated.

Sometimes, inevitably, there are important discrepancies between what is needed or felt to be desirable and what is accessible. So many parents feel obliged to accept what is available as second best, or seek alternative sources of information and reasoning with which to feed the process of making judgements. They attempt to compensate, often in ingenious ways, for the limitations or inadequacies of evidence, or the deliberate control of information and experience, by both children and schools.

A variation on this approach might look at parental judgement as a variable concern involving *people, processes* and *products*. An orientation towards *people* places significance upon the actors involved, their personal qualities and attributes, the relationships they make and are capable of sustaining over time. Within such a focus, talk is likely to be valued highly and positively as an instrument of both learning and relationships, and its acquisition a criterion of what it is to be educated.

A concern with educational *processes*, however, attends largely to observational evidence of activity and relationship. Typically this considers the visible effects of classroom management, such as observed order and apparent activity, together with an increased awareness of aspects of the teaching role that often go unrecorded, such as the supervision of meals or lunchtime activities, preparation for lessons etc.

There is some support for the idea that, as parents become familiar, they are more likely to develop and augment the base of their educational judgements by the additional incorporation of observational evidence. After all, the basis of familiarity for many of the parents provides ample and continuing opportunities to see the life and work of the school *from the inside*. However, the evidence of one's eyes is not always easy to interpret. Neither can most parents bring a systematic body of theory and training to bear upon such experience, even if it were felt to be appropriate.

A concern which necessitates a detailed analysis of educational *products* has been shown to be widespread throughout the present sample of parents. However, this is much more complex than the single and touching faith in school grades and examination results that characterises a potent stereotype of the 'concerned and interested parent', much espoused by the media and teacher lore alike.

ASPECTS OF FAMILIARITY

In this section, the close-up lens is employed freely to portray a variegated picture of parental action and reaction, of initiative, encounter and response. Although some general patterns begin to emerge, the dominant impression is of the range and diversity of attitude and activity which characterise the dealings of parents with their children's schools.

Becoming knowledgeable

There is no doubt that an increasing number of schools make a considerable effort to keep their parents informed about what they are doing. Equally obvious, given the absence of official guidance and support, will be the important variations in the way this is done, both within and between schools. From the parental point of view, too, there will be widely differing assessments about the appropriateness, usability and value of such information.

Most of those parents who choose to become actively involved with their children's schools do have access to more information than is normally the case. They may get standard information earlier, for example, before it is generally made available. They may have access to different or fuller versions of material that is sent or communicated to the parent body as a whole; finally, they may have access to privileged and confidential information that is not generally made available, as a tribute to the special relationships that they are developing with the school and its teachers.

Although it would be tempting to present parental needs in terms of straightforward 'information' (following most official statements, e.g. Plowden, Taylor Report or the most recent Government Green Papers), in practice this is seldom the case. For much information and acquired knowledge are connected with previous experience or create fresh problems of interpretation.

Here, one of the 'Mums' Group' from a council estate primary school describes the educational strategy and value of a canal trip in which she herself participated:

Interviewer. What's the idea of the canal trip? Does it fit into school work?

Mother. Yes, it does really. It's all about the, you know, water-ways and all what happened and how it was all built, so it is an educational thing as well . . . all the locks and how they was built and they also have a book (I don't know whether you've seen it?) And they have this work to do while they're on the boat. It's, um, questions, all, um, 'Who built the first canal?' . . . all what they see and all what they're told. And

51

> I think it's the third day they start this . . . They have books
> on the canal but mostly it's a question of whether they take
> notice or not . . . not just sit on the boat and think it's this . . .
> It's quite a nice holiday and it's an education as well. I learnt
> things that I never thought I would learn.

In the following example, a parent experiences more obvious
difficulty in explaining what they have seen of classroom life, in an
organised way.

> *Father*. Um . . . I would have thought that if you'd got a weak
> teacher, you'd end up with nothing very much happening —
> much pleasanter, I mean we used to sit in regimented lines and
> this sort of thing . . . They've got more windows so there's
> much more light and all this sort of thing. Everything's much
> more informal and, uh, more relaxed and I suppose from that
> point of view the kids feel at home, should *enjoy* school, rather
> than see it as some sort of punishment. But I think that there
> is more tendency to wander about, either physically or
> mentally, than in the old system and I think it requires a lot
> more of the teacher.

The present study shows not only the extent of information-giving
and receiving, but also something of its limitations. For being
knowledgeable about something is not necessarily the same as
understanding what is going on, and making a critical evaluation of
it. So the data reveals how, for many parents, the information stops
short of what is required for a fuller understanding, in crucial ways
and at crucial moments.

Parents' experiences of their children's school need to be
considered in terms of their possible contribution to a deeper
understanding of educative processes and of parental roles within
them, rather than being confined to a superficial picture of what is
going on. Such a distinction is made by parents and teachers alike.
In the first example, an involved mother and a father whose contact
is much more restricted contrast their different pictures of school
life:

> *Interviewer*. So you feel you've got a fairly full picture of what
> is going on in the school, of what's happening?
> *Father*. I wouldn't know about full, I mean I would think that it's
> a very complete surface picture. It appears to be, I mean, I

don't know really but uh, uh, (*pause*) I mean I'm sure there
must be all sorts of stresses and strains within the school,
which one never really hears about.

Mother. I personally feel I have quite a good picture of what's
going on in the school, but I think it's because I, I've made
the effort to *get into* the school and involve myself in it.

In the second example, a home/school liaison teacher talks about
some of the consequences of close and regular contact with parents:

Community teacher. They know what's going on because we talk
about, you know, the school jubilee plans, and they know
about things before the general letter goes out. And quite a few
of them come in and do work on a Tuesday afternoon for the
teachers.

Interviewer. Does that apply to the educational life of the school
as well? Do those mums get a clear or different picture of what
goes on in classrooms?

Community teacher. Well they're not *working* in classrooms in
the main, but I think they perhaps do get a clearer idea because
they often ask me about things, uh and if their child has a *little
problem*, they wouldn't come up to school specially for,
they'll just mention it to me or, could I have a word with the
class teacher. So I think things must be clearer to them,
perhaps not basic educational policy but more general things.

On further analysis of this particular group it becomes possible
to make and sustain the following distinctions:

Familiar with	*Not familiar with*
Individual teachers	Educational philosophies and rationales
Everyday school routines	Educational policies
The recurring events of the school calendar and curriculum	Teaching strategies (though sometimes familiar with specific *techniques*)

Many of the 'familiar parents' in this study have access (as either
an explicit or incidental part of their involvement) to the *working life*
of the school, with the special consequences that this entails. Such
opportunities to get *inside* the school, to see how it operates behind
the scenes, may provide access to classroom life (viewed through

windows or sometimes more directly by working alongside teachers), the life of corridors and classrooms, occasionally even incorporating life in protected zones like the staffroom or the school office. Such opportunities are seldom available to parents as a whole, and then only in tantalisingly brief, unsystematic ways.

What very few parents of any kind get, however, are explanations of what the school is doing, and more particularly how and why it is doing it. Even the most involved parents in this sample have very few opportunities to test out their growing understanding of educational matters, through the questioning of professionals. Consequently, although many of the parents in the sample appear to be better informed about life in their children's schools, its routines and organisation, they do not necessarily derive a clearer *understanding* from the things they observe and experience. Yet, for better or worse, most of them know enough to know that things cannot always be taken at face value!

So the sample contains many parents who appear to be in the very process of struggling to come to terms with their familiarity, and its consequences both for a deeper understanding and for parental action. This activity (which incorporates many important variations) is here characterised as a general view of what is going on and a proven method of checking it out. Such a process might eventually lead to the formulation of a personalised accounting system or frameworks to 'explain' behaviour and events. It owes as much to a concern for developing an approach to the collection and handling of evidence, as to a growing capacity to organise finished fragments of understanding into a coherent whole.

However, it is possible to overstate the development of *rational* understanding, based upon an increasing tendency to weigh up arguments and evidence, and to ignore very different approaches. In our material, for instance, contrasting approaches are provided by a guide mistress and a local authority foster mother of many years' standing. The insight they have developed is based not on the development of a theory or an accounting system. It derives from a more *intuitive* orientation, supported by generalisation from the experience of their own and other people's children, rather than from a working knowledge of schools and classrooms.

Another thread that runs across the interview material suggests that a developing familiarity implies some movement at least in the direction of a wider or a deeper view of educational processes. Such a view often derives from a growing conviction that educational behaviour cannot be understood as a series of separate, self-contained incidents, but as a developing process that occurs in a series of dynamic and influential contexts.

Here, 'becoming familiar' can be seen in terms both of taking opportunities to examine some of the contextual features of educational situations, relationships and processes, as well as suggesting the need to extend one's perspective to consider new features and other forms of evidence.

The active pursuit of concern

As a general rule, parents appear willing to take a great deal on trust and show considerable patience and restraint when things are not going well. For a significant number, however, there are occasions when school explanations or suggested remedies do not seem to make sense or to be appropriate solutions. At such times parents will sooner or later feel compelled to intervene, in what they feel are the best interests of their children, even if that jeopardises their existing relationships with the school — a move which parents do not make lightly.

Our work with parents has highlighted their very different reactions by identifying two contrasting strategies.

'The full frontal'

Here, parents are sure-footed about their conviction that something is wrong, whether or not this conflicts with official judgements. Indeed, the persistence of a school in imposing its own definitions, or in maintaining that there *is* no problem, may serve to stiffen a parent's resolve or to trigger committed action. For example, school judgements about achievement in different areas such as spelling or reading, or a proposal to send a child to a special school, have been proferred in blatant contradiction not only of parents' knowledge in general, but the direct, highly accessible evidence of their own eyes.

The determination and persistence of parents to pursue what they feel to be in the best interests of their children, often in the face of continuing obstacles placed by the school, can yield spectacular results which vindicate those efforts. In this group, a boy who was to go to a special school ends up with 'O' level passes! However, in the present account, such cases serve rather to illustrate a problem-solving route to a wider understanding of educational institutions and processes.

Mother. My eldest boy is dyslexic. Now you know that causes me a lot of problems throughout education, erm. We moved around the London area quite a bit and their idea was they either gave him, they put into a, a class of, a *remedial* class which wasn't good for him because he's got a fairly high IQ erm and that wasn't good for him. Er, they then thought of sending him to a special school because he wasn't settling in the remedial and they couldn't understand why. Er, *that* we stopped, we wasn't having that . . . Erm, we went to Bournemouth . . . they, they just gave him paper and pencil and let him draw his way through sums so I stopped him going to school . . . er so I had that kind of performance. When we came here, this is one thing that you know I'm all for the school for this reason, erm, as far as that boy's concerned they were marvellous, they really were . . . Er, they, everyone, was aware of Steven's problems but they didn't make it noticeable in front of the children er, and they did get someone from the University that came and tested him you know in various ways and he confirmed that he was dyslexic. He came out of here with three 'O' levels. I mean when he came into school he really, he would only read to *me* . . . I mean I went through the Ladybird books and he could read to me but that was it. If anyone walked in the room he couldn't read. Er, he came out with three 'O' levels, he's now just finished his apprenticeship for a tool maker. (*Interviewer*. Mm, fantastic.) So, and he was, really was quite bad.

'The nagging problem'

Here, as the contrast with the previous type implies, the generation of anxiety is diffused over a longer period of time. Indeed, part of the problem lies in the fact that the nature and definition of the issues are not clear-cut. It may be, reasons the parent, that there isn't a problem. The anxiety that is felt may be thought to be misplaced, or exaggerated. But however the parent attempts to rationalise the anxiety, it won't go away.

Typically, a strategy that grows as a response to the 'nagging problem' will include:

• An initial (usually unsatisfactory) checking out of anxieties against those of teachers or other parents. This is done informally rather than as the result of a direct visit, which is too threatening at this stage.

• The monitoring or checking out of relevant evidence over a period of time. This is often done in a very painstaking and detailed way, e.g. the regular examination of homework or of a particular teacher's marking.

• The search for comparative evidence of different kinds, or alternative sources of expertise or illumination with which to challenge those of the school.

• Above all, a strategy which is characterised by extended and detailed introspection and cud-chewing, until a clearer understanding of the problem and a confidence in one's own efforts to challenge the school effectively begin to emerge.

In the present sample, such strategies were used most in relation to marking policies, different versions of maths education and the capacity of mixed-ability grouping to challenge more able pupils (from the parents of both primary- and secondary-aged children).

Father. . . . and so next time round, you seem much more conscious of the next child, that you're making even more effort to make sure you're keeping tabs on the situation. But it's concerning . . . How can you have a blow by blow account, day by day, week by week. You're dependent on, first of all, you know, if anything's going wrong. For the first few weeks the child won't say anything, maybe one or two odd remarks and then over a period of time you build up a picture that something isn't too good, say maths or English. But you've got to allow a certain amount of time to elapse before you actually do something consciously about it. 'Cos, I, I wouldn't go willy-nilly into school. I'd have to be absolutely convinced and that it wasn't just a whim of one of my kids, 'cos kids sometimes spin tales. But by the time you've been completely convinced and you feel, you know, strong enough to go into school and make a point about it, there may be (unless it's something out of the ordinary) three months that have elapsed at least, haven't they, and perhaps a good part of the year, before the situation's righted. Um, and I'm much more aware of that. Uh, with me, I've got one in the sixth, and I'm learning all the time.

'Becoming like them'

The study of familiar parents contains evidence of joint effort between home and school, widespread examples of shared concern for the education and welfare of individuals and, often, a self-critical appraisal of each other's effort. Whilst research and practice within the rhetoric of partnership have tended to overstate the evidence of mutual support and collaboration between home and school, there is a danger that we will do the opposite! This would be to overlook the obvious pleasure and satisfaction which many accounts contain, based upon the educational support which many familiar parents have felt able to provide for their children and also from their general contacts with school teachers. This even applies to those who work in schools, often on a part-time, poorly-paid basis, such as the school meals and welfare assistants. It is present in the warm accounts of educational trips and joint enterprises, and in the rather frequent use of the pronoun 'we' to describe such efforts.

There is little doubt that many of those parents who choose to have extended contact with their children's teachers and schools, come to identify more closely with their goals and activities. For those whose contacts may have critical, or even hostile origins, either through the school's treatment of their children or at the level of philosophy, policy or practice, this can represent a considerable shift, even if it is sometimes only grudgingly acknowledged!

There is little doubt, too, that those forms of contact which provide a working knowledge of schools and classrooms through offering direct involvement and experiences, are likely to bring about changes of attitude and possibly behaviour, often in a dramatic and convincing way. It remains necessary to ask, however, whether the changes operate in one direction only or whether, as has been previously claimed with considerable justification, this only applies when parents act within the school goals and on its terms.

The accounts of familiar parents contain plenty of examples of differing, apparently contradictory, evidence. On the one hand there is evidence of schools (even those claiming to be egalitarian and open) which use involvement programmes as a way of promoting chosen, potentially supportive parents to a position closer to the school pulse. The material contains clear accounts of parents being socialised into the school culture and of the incorporation of professional values, methods and techniques by parents into their parenting. (This issue is examined, through the other end of the telescope, in Chapter 6 'Defining the Boundaries', where several teachers claim that their teaching has been transformed through the process of being a parent.)

Similarly, the supplementary fieldwork contains, in written materials and headteacher interviews, the apparent view that the 'problem' of home background can be solved not only by making poor homes more like the better ones *in kind*, but also by making parenting more like teaching, through the consistent application of relevant theories, rules and procedures. The process of educational colonisation, however, is by no means confined to the field of home/school relations!

> *Mother.* I think, I think I understand better the way they teach them erm, because when the kids used to . . . bring work home I used to think 'How the hell do they teach them that?' . . . and, er, I mean I never did that like that. But now I've come into school and I talk to the teachers and they explain how they do teach them, it's a lot better 'cos then I can help them more because I know that's the way yer do it.

However, there is even stronger evidence that, for many parents, as familiarity with schools and classrooms develops, and understanding grows, the experience of involvement tends to:

• sharpen their sense of parenting, rather than blurring its distinctions from teaching;
• promote a positive view of school life which nevertheless is sanguine about its weaknesses and limitations;
• serve as a stimulus to the development of home-made, compensatory strategies to tackle perceived difficulties, as they affect their own children.

Schools that we have worked with differ widely in their capacity and willingness to even recognise such possibilities, let alone work actively to bring about their growth and development. But there is, in our view, much untapped potential here within a rationale where parenting and teaching are brought to bear upon one another, constructively but critically. This needs to focus upon a collaboration that recognises the complementary natures and deep underlying tensions that inevitably characterise relationships between the respective institutions of home and school.

A wider view

Finally, the 'process of becoming familiar' has claims to be considered as an 'educative' experience in its own right. This might apply equally to a consideration of its purposes, its content or its effects. So, for example, some parents come to value the acquisition of certain knowledge and skills, confident in their own judgement, or the development of understanding, *as important and satisfying in themselves*, rather than just for any instrumental benefits that can be passed on to their children.

The movement to a wider view of educational processes and of their own part in them is often characterised by an increasing willingness to consider arguments and evidence in a variety of forms, accompanied by a need to discuss and to reflect. Where such activity develops into a coherent theory or accounting system, it is unlikely to be confined to specific issues and situations, but to see these as located against a wider background stemming from the problematic nature of parenting and teaching in contemporary society:

> *Mother.* I think a lot of parents do it without realising that you're
> doing it. Just the fact that you show interest in what they're
> doing, and erm, you know, sort of become involved. Not to
> take over. I think it's important that you don't take over . . .
> they've been doing a project on Nuthall in Georgian times . . .
> and I've learnt more from Chris, but by Chris asking me . . .
> he's coming home, and he's said, 'Do you know, mum, that
> there are so many coalminers, so many so-and-so's.' Now all
> really Chris's been doing is involving me — I think by being
> involved, and being willing to be involved, it's helped him,
> because then he's been even more interested . . . but just
> listening, yeah, I think you help. But I think you help almost
> subconsciously. But I think by being interested, you make
> them want to find out even more. Not necessarily saying,
> 'Right, get your book out, we'll have so-and-so done', you
> know, I think you've got to be available . . .
>
> . . . but I don't think you ever think, it, it must be educational
> to a degree . . . I don't think you ever set a time of day aside
> and think, 'Right, we'll do some clever stuff!' you know.

'BECOMING FAMILIAR': GETTING IT IN PERSPECTIVE

Many, but by no means all, of the parents who become familiar with their children's schools are drawn by a wish to support their work or to become more fully involved. The origins of much of this activity are reinforced by its voluntary nature or, in the case of ancillary workers, the very different combinations of shop-floor solidarity and the well-known capacity of schools to bind their members together as part of a symbolic order — 'of being in it together'. This sense of belonging to a shared concern often incorporates parents whose early contact and involvement was sparked off by strong criticism of particular teachers, policies or practices. For being drawn into the life and work of the school often requires an implicit acceptance of the school's philosophy and ethos. It invites support, consensus and agreement.

Against this, however, there are instances where the opposite happens. For such parents familiarity does, indeed, breed contempt! Here, knowing the school provides the exposure of its weaknesses, or the confirmation of one's own prejudices or worst suspicions.

Similarly, whilst many of the parents are willing to accept school judgements and actions on professional matters, greater familiarity and involvement leads others to act more independently and on their own terms. This involves the active pursuit of argument and evidence but also, more ambitiously, the challenging of some school definitions. What most of these parents have in common is a willingness to see the school progress of their children as an appropriate and legitimate arena for intervention and parental influence. This contrasts markedly with a passive fatalism about home/school matters that we have often come across in other people's work.

The familiarity of parents who have had considerable dealings with their children's schools, for different reasons and in widely differing ways, is hard-earned. It contrasts sharply with the problems of parents of children starting in a new school, struggling to form an early impression, or those relating to children who attend schools with very limited opportunities for communication, contact and involvement. Familiar parents, by definition, are more likely to have given consideration to, and often taken part in, discussion of their experience with teachers and other parents. There is evidence to suggest that, as parents become more experienced at dealing with schools and more familiar with the problems of doing so, they become more discriminating. They attend to information and evidence in a more selective and focused way, tailoring what they

61

seek to match their needs. This applies both to specific, child-related problems and to the more general understanding of educational issues, although the two are obviously linked.

However, it would be all to easy to overstate this and to gloss over a number of important tensions and problems that are firmly established. For many of these parents, as for many others, the gains represented are very limited, or potential rather than actual. Whilst many schools increasingly attempt to communicate with parents about what they are doing, they also regard this as essentially a one-way, non-problematic process. So, whilst parents may have been informed about changes in organisational routine, for example, this is less frequently matched by a corresponding understanding of classroom life, for the conditions for acquiring such an understanding have not been met.

Schools often fail to communicate in terms that parents are able to make sense of, or use effectively; neither do they give adequate attention to the *ways* in which this might be done or to the implications of both for professional training and teacher development. But unless parents are able to develop some kind of accounting system, through opportunities to see, to discuss and to experience, information, *in itself*, is unlikely to have consequences for children's schooling.

Taken together, the issues raised by listening to this particular cross-section of parents emphasise two important and recurring themes:

The problematic nature of communication — There's more to it than meets the eye!

The problems of opening-up institutions and relationships — Some problems will be solved, but others will just as certainly take their place!

As parents become more familiar with their children's schools, they will form a clearer picture of the collective skills and efforts of the head and his or her staff. But they will also, sooner or later, become aware of glaring inefficiencies in the system or of professional ignorance on the part of particular teachers; they will develop a clearer idea of their opposition to particular ideas and practices, and qualify their support for others, either at the level of ideology and belief or as the result of critical experience of ideas in practice.

Opening up schools to parents and the wider community also allows the possibility, perhaps even encourages, parental support and intervention. Such a view entails the recognition of the special features of parental perspectives as a source of strength and confidence and as a springboard for action. It also recognises that parents will increasingly consider such intervention to be both necessary and legitimate.

A a result of their developing familiarity, many familiar parents seem willing and able to challenge the school's

- definition of the problem;
- proposed course of action (or perceived inaction!);
- methods/ways of doing things;
- evaluation of the consequences of a particular decision or of a particular course of action.

Professional perspectives tend to stress the application of theories and principles, rule-based policies and systematic forms of treatment. The strategies of familiar parents, by contrast, are negotiated through relationships with known individuals. They are therefore based upon the specific features of the particular case under examination. Whilst the capacity of parents to intervene effectively can be related to a growing understanding of the issues, it also incorporates a need to build person-oriented relationships through which action can be formulated and from which the confidence to act can be fostered. This can either be as a response to positive initiatives from the school, or occur in spite of their absence!

Familiarity with schools enables many parents to place their closely observed pictures of individuals, developed within a range of family settings, against the background of the institutional arrangements that govern the life of schools. As a response to the problems that will inevitably arise, many of the parents in this sample appear to have been able:

- to put pressure on schools and teachers in ways that bring about a redefinition of the problem;
- to borrow from the resources and skills of the professional repertoire ideas and practices that can be adapted for use *by parents themselves*; or
- to develop, for themselves, counter-strategies and techniques, to achieve what *parents* see as desirable ends.

SOME GENERAL POINTERS

The study of particular groups of parents and their dealings with their children's schools highlights a number of general concerns, each of which contains pointers for the development of thinking and practice (which are taken up in a more detailed, practical way in Part Three). These concerns, however, reinforce the need for both new attitudes and new ways of working.

(i) *The development of practical arrangements for effective communication between parents, teachers and pupils lies at the heart of good home/school relationships.*

The development of genuinely responsive communication is much more than a technical matter and involves a considerable shift from the patterns of thinking and practice that are currently widespread. It certainly goes beyond the 'official' view, enshrined in legislation and government reports, which sees communication only in terms of a one-way flow of basic, factual information.

What is required is communication which is wide-ranging and varied in form, which acknowledges widely differing parental views and experience, as well as their different needs and preferences. It will attempt to go beyond a willingness to inform, to encourage the development of understanding. To achieve this, it will need to incorporate varied opportunities for parents to see, to discuss and, above all, to *experience*, as part of a continuing dialogue between themselves and teachers. This necessarily involves pupils, although they are often overlooked in practice.

Against this broader approach, the present efforts of many schools seem unnecessarily limited in purpose, restricted in scope and unimaginative in style.

(ii) *Effective basic communication needs to be backed up by a range of appropriate opportunities for parents to participate in their children's schooling*, as part of an important joint venture that has serious implications for the future lives of pupils.

There is now a rich and varied repertoire of ideas and experience available to schools and teachers, which embodies practical ways of sharing responsibility, of developing mutual forms of support and joint action. What is less widespread is an appreciation of its value and a will to make such ideas work. On the other hand parents (like teachers!) have widely differing, even contradictory, views about the ways and the extent to which they should become involved with schools. They certainly should not be made to feel guilty because their views do not fit with those that prevail, either generally or in particular schools. Parents can make a powerful case for not becoming actively involved in their children's schools.

Above all, parental views are modified by their *experience of communication and involvement*. A good general illustration is provided by the transfer of children from primary to secondary schools, which represents a fundamental shift for pupils and parents alike. Each institution has its own strengths and weaknesses. So parents often experience great discontinuity from one class teacher to the next in the primary school; this is followed by the displacement and marginalisation of home/school matters in the secondary school, by the pressures of subject teaching or its reduction to the bureaucratic mechanisms of marks and reports.

(iii) *Schools need to recognise, support and strengthen the crucial role of parents as educators.*
As with all of these general statements, this cannot be done without listening to parents and taking their perspectives and experience into account. Schools have an important role to play in encouraging parents to develop their own strategies as educators and in helping them to achieve the confidence to implement them. In practical terms, efforts to do this have probably been concentrated too much at the early years end of the age-range.

(iv) *Parents represent a valuable, but often unacknowledged, resource which could be tapped to great effect in the education of children and young people.*
Any group of parents represents a considerable collection of knowledge, skill and experience; there are many things that parents know and can do, that stem from their backgrounds, their work, their leisure pursuits and, above all, their experience of life. It seems a squandering of valuable resources not to be able to see this, although some schools have done so, either in a relatively systematic way, through some kind of inventory, or more informally. Sometimes when there is a high level of parental participation in the life of a school, such resources are right under the noses of teachers and so get overlooked!

The study of 'familiar parents' provides a vivid picture of home/school beliefs and practices, located in what are generally felt to be favourable and supportive circumstances. Unlike many accounts in this area, however, which are drunk on the rhetoric, this view has a sharp edge, suggesting both the challenges and the opportunities of trying to communicate more effectively with parents and of trying to involve them more fully in the life and work of the school.

For opening up school identifies large areas of potential support and uncovers considerable untapped resources of many kinds. It also invites risk and exposure, with new opportunities for parents to pass comment and make judgements. It is no easy path or soft option, posing, as it does, a formidable challenge to schools and teachers but one which, in our view, cannot and should not be avoided.

6

Defining the Boundaries

Every country in Europe, and Britain is no exception, places the legal responsibility for children's education in the hands of their parents or guardians. The 1944 Act confirming the parental duty to educate said this was to be met by attendance at school or otherwise. The existence of the 'or otherwise' clause makes it clear that school is not the only place where education takes place; moreover the case histories of parents who have fought successfully to educate their children at home shows that education is not mediated only by professionally trained teachers. Legally, then, if rarely in practice, the boundaries between home and school and parents and teachers are blurred.

However, the development of schooling and the gradual introduction of compulsory training for all teachers has led to general acceptance of professional control over education and the belief that teachers alone possess the skills, knowledge and expertise to educate children. The functions of the family and the school came to be seen as separate, the one concerned with socialisation, the other with education. Such boundaries in role were denoted in physical terms by the classic notice 'No parents beyond this point' and in more oblique ways, as referred to by the parent who felt she'd been told 'let us do the teaching, you do the parenting'.

However, these boundaries have been challenged recently by the growth of the accountability movement and increasing emphasis on parental rights, for example, to express a preference as to their children's schools and receive information. The development of home reading schemes and similar strategies further blurs the demarcation between parenting and teaching and opens up for debate the question of just what is professional knowledge, expertise and skill. All of these changes challenge the traditional autonomy of the teacher and redefine the role of parents, and yet the legacy of past boundaries remains.

For many years the problem underlying home/school relationships was perceived to be that of social class. Put crudely the theory was that if only working-class parents could be helped to become more like middle-class parents, children's achievements would be equalised and better understanding would exist between schools and homes. This definition of the problem has now been widened to include race, and difficulties between schools and ethnic minority parents are explained in terms of different cultural backgrounds and perceptions of education. There is a familiar ring to the infant teacher's plea, 'If only Asian parents understood the importance of play!' We would not wish to deny that class, race and indeed gender are important barriers that divide teachers and parents as much as they do society as a whole. However, conceptualising home/school relationships in this way leaves unexamined the assumption that middle-class parents are successful in their dealings with schools and that this is explained by:

- possession of appropriate knowledge and information;
- shared values with the schooling system;
- confidence with which to relate to teachers.

In other words, for them boundaries are almost non-existent.

But is the higher educational achievement of their children a justification for the belief that relationships with schools are unproblematic for middle-class parents? Teachers have clearly had doubts — the 'pushy' or 'interfering' parent is as much part of staff-room lore as the apathetic or uninterested one.

Intuitively we had long felt that easy explanations and assumptions about the successful relationships middle-class parents had with schools did not accord with our own experience as parents, nor with that of colleagues and friends. So we felt a growing sense of puzzlement at the idea that making 'them' more like 'us' would dissolve the barriers between home and school. It was this that led us to want to look more closely at the experiences of parents who fitted the criteria of possessing knowledge, shared values and, presumably, confidence. Which group of parents fitted this description better than those who were themselves teachers? A growing realisation that the literature on home and school conceptualises parents and teachers separately, crystallised the decision that a study of teacher-parents was long overdue. Through listening to these parents we hope to shed further light on the nature of the boundaries between home and school; in particular we explore the ways in which parents who are fellow-professionals experience contact with their own children's schools. What happens when the lay/professional barrier is apparently dissolved? Are the explanations that support the view that middle-class parents are successful in their dealings with school valid?

KNOWLEDGE AND INFORMATION

One basis of teachers' professionalism is a claim to particular knowledge that the lay parent does not possess. Teacher-parents make clear distinctions between two kinds of knowledge about education. On the one hand they know about the schooling system as a whole. They know how schools are organised and where authority and power is based. They often have wider knowledge about particular schools, gained from the 'teacher Mafia' as one described it, and they use such knowledge of schools and the system when choosing schools for their children.

> I think it's been very useful in that you can quickly sum up an educational system — again, I think selection of schools, you know what you — or you hope you know what will suit your children best . . . and I think when it comes to career choice it helps, because as I said, we tried hard for Lisa to keep the options open.

On the other hand they have knowledge about the particular age-range they teach and the subject-matter they possess, however narrow or broad that might be. This second kind of knowledge, however, is seen as being far less useful than the first kind; it is only of value when their children are at a particular stage of education or studying the subject they are familiar with.

> There was the teacher there who knew that we were teachers, there was a hesitancy in trying to enlarge on what I wanted to know, almost as if to say 'Well, you should know about it', you know, but which wasn't the case because to me it was a different world and it was my, our child.

Or as a biology teacher in a comprehensive school put it:

I know next to nothing about infant teaching, so I couldn't go, I'd never dream of going to put my spoke in. Now perhaps when the girls come up to secondary education perhaps I'll be different then.

We are reminded therefore that professional knowledge is itself partial and incomplete. No single teacher has the knowledge that all teachers possess and no parent can possibly have the knowledge that teachers as a whole have. There are parallels here with other professions; medicine, for example, is both a general and a specialist field and the lay patient may have knowledge of parts of the field just as the heart surgeon may be quite ignorant about gynaecology.

Even claims that teachers' professionalism lies in their knowledge of child development and of general patterns of learning and behaviour are only partially true. Much of this knowledge is acquired not through training but through the experience of teaching children in schools, and teachers who move to a different kind of area testify to the new learning they have to do about children. Moreover any teacher who has taken children away from school on a residential trip tells how teachers learn so much more about children in this setting. Parents, on the other hand, may not know how their children behave at school but they do know them intimately. They know 'what makes them tick' and 'their funny little ways' and what kind of motivation they need 'to get them going'. Indeed teacher-parents emphasise that they felt the experience of being a parent has given them more understanding of children in general and changed their approach to teaching.

I think Ben and Dan made me much more sensitive to kids' feelings, much more aware of the way in which schools make learning unexciting and dull and boring and a drudge — it *broadens* your perspective an awful lot about children.

I think it had a tremendous influence — it made me far more sensitive to their *happiness* — I think it made me a very much more *sympathetic* teacher, I found it very difficult suddenly to holler at children any more.

It appears, then, that teachers' knowledge about children in general and parents' more particular and specialist knowledge about their own children can complement and enrich each other's perspectives. Just as parents who work alongside teachers in classrooms can appreciate more the wide range of children's needs and abilities that teachers have to meet, so teachers who can appreciate the parental perspective find their attitude to parents changes.

> I'm far more understanding, because you understand the problems that *you've* experienced with your own children. I often say, 'Look, I've got three children myself. I know what you *mean*' . . . unless you've been a parent you don't *know* what the parent feels, but you do if you've had a family because you've felt it yourself.

To explain the lay/professional relationship as one characterised by professional knowledge and lay ignorance seems to us, then, a simplification of what is in reality a complex issue in which the nature of knowledge and ignorance is itself problematic.

It is, then, not so much particular knowledge that teacher-parents value but rather their understanding of the educational system in general.

> I've used professional knowledge to chase things through, I mean both Barry and Jane have discovered that it's very difficult to con us about what's going on at school 'cos I *know* what goes on in schools.

The problematic nature of professional knowledge is also shown by the way teacher-parents react in different ways when their own specialism is in question. Some of them see such knowledge as a handicap:

> I've had to be careful when he was doing his own History homework that I did not in any way involve myself because I had quite different views of how the subject should be taught. James was taught on dictated notes which I thought was appalling, erm, on the other hand I taught 'O' level and not 'A' level, therefore, you know, it would be different, but I kept myself very much to 'How is he doing? Satisfactory, oh good', and didn't ask for very much more.

We have here a hint that knowledge alone is not sufficient to remove barriers between teachers and parents, despite this parent's explanation that her own knowledge was partial. Further insight is offered by a secondary school teacher of English who describes how she learnt a successful strategy after experiencing what she described as 'whitewashes' to her problems with her child's primary school.

> I think I've tackled it in a better way in that I did monitor the progress, detail it down so that they knew there was really no argument . . . Sarah and English Literature and English Language at 'O' levels had an appallingly bad teacher who did very little work with them and I monitored the homework and the written work over a period of time, a term, I think, and put it down in great detail and sent a covering letter with it to the head, and pointed out that as an English teacher I felt that I had some professional expertise if you like, and wrote to point out that I was very unhappy about the teaching that was going on and in fact I got a very full letter back from the head, though obviously it had to go through the head of department — really I suppose whitewashing — but nevertheless after that the teaching did improve.

Although this parent used her professional knowledge to *support* and *justify* her action to the school, her strategy of carefully monitoring what was happening is one that we found 'familiar' parents using (as described in the previous chapter). What emerges it seems to us is not that content knowledge is a particular advantage but that understanding what might be called 'the rules of the game' together with the confidence to tackle the school, leads to an experience of success. For some of these parents the school is an institution governed by a sense of professional rationality, in other words it will respond to systematic and 'objective' evidence. However, not all teacher-parents have the same attitude (as the History teacher showed) and we shall explore later their various stances towards contact with their children's schools.

Although professional knowledge of the content of the curriculum does not seem a significant influence for teacher-parents, they do nevertheless display a confidence in their ability to help their children with school work, regardless of their particular background. This sense of competence appears to stem not so much from their professionality as from their own capacities as educated people. Thus the infant head could help her 15-year-old son with his homework regardless of its content, the biology teacher assisted her 7-year-old daughter with maths, while a primary teacher read the 'O' level English texts with her daughter. Interestingly they made clear distinctions between what they saw as 'helping' and the act of teaching. The dynamics of the parent/child relationship is a factor here as many of their children resisted receiving any action that could be termed direct instruction.

I could help at home and I did indirectly by giving her notes and finding her books and letting her read them. She would never let me teach her directly but I did in fact provide a lot of help.

David has made clear distinctions in his mind as to what he will *allow* his mother to do and what he won't, and teaching him to read is the teacher's task, it's not mother's task.

The next chapter explores in much more detail the role of the parent as educator but it is worth noting here that for these parents teaching is conceptualised as formal, planned and systematic instruction whereas in the home their educative role is much more incidental, follows the child's lead and is seen as facilitative and supportive. In considering the boundary between parenting and teaching, then, a key concept appears to be the nature of the relationship between adult and child. Teachers in school have to be professional in the sense of being impartial and fair in their dealings with all pupils, whereas parents are allowed to have an emotional bond and can afford to respond to the individual and idiosyncratic nature of their children.

Finally, in reconsidering the question of the place of knowledge in the lay/professional relationship, through listening to teacher-parents, two conclusions emerge. Firstly, detailed knowledge of curriculum content that teachers possess is not necessarily a barrier between home and school and does not seem to be a requisite if parents wish to be involved with their children's learning. One implication of this is that schools opening up the curriculum to parents need to put less emphasis on particular content and more on broader learning strategies that parents can assist children with. Secondly, the kind of knowledge that these parents find useful is their understanding of the educational system as a whole. This gives them the ability to make choices based on adequate information; to understand both the limitations that class sizes and scant resources place upon schools and the real weaknesses that some teachers have; to know the structure of the school's hierarchy and the appropriate person to approach with a problem. This kind of knowledge is not inaccessible to other parents, as the study of familiar parents (Chapter 5) showed. Nevertheless, we reiterate the view that was expressed there; while greater understanding can lead to a more supportive co-operative relationship it can also challenge and expose schools to sharper questioning and more open disagreement. Whether this happens or not, though, seems to be dependent on factors other than the possession of knowledge as such, as we now see when looking at teacher-parents stances towards contact with schools.

TEACHER-PARENT STANCES TOWARDS THEIR CHILDREN'S SCHOOLS

Traditionally the boundaries between home and school have been set by schools themselves. The power to determine the nature and extent of contact between parents and teachers has rested with the professionals who have also, in endeavouring to protect and enhance their own role and autonomy, ascribed to the parent a marginal and peripheral role in the education of their children. An era of minimal contact gave way to one where parents were expected to be supportive and co-operative but not to criticise or question. Now, for the kind of reasons outlined in the Introduction to this book, parents have moved closer to the centre of the educational stage and the balance of power between the professional teacher and the lay parent is shifting. However, moves to give parents in general more power through choice of schools, membership of governing bodies and access to more information have not necessarily yet altered the attitudes of parents and teachers towards each other. The relationship of the individual parent and teacher is strongly influenced by the biographical history each has and part of this will involve their perceptions of their role as professional and lay person. Changing roles inevitably leads to tension and conflict. The parent whose model of a teacher is the authoritative instructor may perceive the child-centred informal teacher as 'not a proper teacher'. The professional trained to regard parents as ignorant or interfering amateurs will find it hard to cope with parents who question decisions or expect a say in school policy. We outlined earlier factors that have been put forward to explain middle-class parents' apparently successful dealings with schools and one of these is the idea that they possess the necessary confidence to meet teachers on a more equal basis. This idea has an appealing simplicity and is often used to sustain a class-based theory of the barriers between home and school. But how true is it? Teacher-parents are the parents most likely to meet fellow-professionals as equals. What does listening to them tell us about teacher/parent relationships? Despite their shared membership of the teaching profession, what emerges is the *variety* of stances they adopt.

Maintaining a low profile

Far from being an advantage, many teacher-parents regard shared professionalism as a handicap in relation to their children's schooling. Very aware of the potential for tension and disagreement they adopt a conscious policy of maintaining a low profile, even to the extent of not disclosing they are fellow teachers; as one put it, 'I'd rather they didn't know that I'm a professional — I want to be treated as "just a parent".' These parents' strategy of non-interference is to 'wait and see', to give the school the benefit of the doubt, to reserve their judgement, hold back from questioning and consciously avoid criticism or interference. Sometimes this reticence is explained as due to feelings of professional solidarity:

> You felt you couldn't argue with her, you didn't want to put her on the spot, you didn't want to make her feel inadequate but what can you do? You can't pick holes in somebody's teaching and just kind of cut her to pieces. So I'm just holding back and not saying anything, just listening most of the time.

Sometimes, however, these parents hold views about teachers' actions that are echoed by many other parents and they hold back criticisms for fear their child will be victimised:

> I was *very* aware of the power that she was going to have over my child, so I didn't dare push it 'cos I knew there were a thousand and one ways she could get back through the child.

This illustrates another aspect of the different nature of the power teachers and parents have. Both have power over the child but the teacher's power is supported by the institutional structure of the school; the parent in a much closer and more intimate relationship is more open to the child's influence: 'I had the message very firmly put that I was not to cause them any embarrassment whatsoever, "Don't you go saying things!"'

For parents determined not to intervene, other than by helping their child at home, there are very few strategies left if things are perceived as wrong. The only solution to real difficulties that enables the position of non-interference to be sustained is the action of removing a child from a particular school. Even here the decision will often rest on their perception of the child's capacity to cope with the school rather than their own views on the education it offers: 'He is *not* desperately unhappy, it's the least of the evils, if he *were* desperately unhappy then I would probably take him out of the school altogether.'

Accepting the way things are

That increased knowledge and understanding does not inevitably mean challenge and conflict is shown by a group of teacher-parents who are quite willing to accept the authority of the school and the judgements of the teacher. Listening to these parents talk one can almost forget they are themselves teachers: 'I didn't bother, I considered that he was with teachers who'd been trained and therefore he would be getting on all right.' Even where professional knowledge is referred to as a way of judging schools they are content to accept the school's way of doing things even if they do not agree with it:

> *Parent.* I felt the whole approach was not as I would prefer it to be.
> *Interviewer.* So what did you do about that, as a parent?
> *Parent.* Nothing really, except moan at home. I didn't feel that I could, er, challenge the teacher at all. I felt I had to accept it, and I did accept it, but I was put out.

These parents are quite willing to leave education to their fellow-professionals and provided all seems well there is no particular reason to get involved. Judgements on their children's progress are made by reference to their behaviour at home and teachers' assurances at parents' evenings. Indeed if all is well then they feel no need to visit the school and even attendance at school functions is often no more than a formality. Should there be a problem, any intervention is done as tactfully and in as non-aggressive a way as possible.

We'd have to be pushed. I think, our children would have to be more than just a little unhappy at school, for us to actually go in. It has happened once in one of the kid's careers, he reckoned he was being bullied and we did actually go in and had a chat . . . did it very informally, very quietly.

Welcome though many teachers would find such acceptance and understanding it is also salutary to realise that many of these successful products of the educational system share the same fears and anxieties expressed by non-professional parents. This comes through in frequent references to the importance of the welcome extended at open evenings, and comments on teachers 'who smile', 'treat you as a human being', 'are approachable', and 'lighten the atmosphere'. Confidence is certainly not universal in the middle class! 'When I had to go to the first comp. evening I felt almost threatened that they were going to say something nasty about my daughter.'

What can I do to help?

Many teacher-parents help their children at home in a variety of ways, such as compensating for aspects they feel are lacking at school, providing books, sharing interests and assisting with homework. Some, however, specifically negotiate their relationship with schools through adopting the stance of being a helper. They have few inhibitions about visiting the school or raising issues because it is always done in the context of asking how they can help with the problem rather than to make criticisms of the policies or teaching. In this way they convince themselves that they will be able to obtain the best out of an imperfect educational system which they have no wish or need to challenge and also avoid the charge of interfering or being a nuisance. This theme of helping is accompanied by a stress on good relationships as a way of avoiding conflict, and so the parent will attend school functions and respond to requests for help in order to establish personal contact with teachers. From this basis it then becomes easier to deal with potential problems:

> *Interviewer.* If one of your girls came home and you got the idea she was having a deal of difficulty with her maths, what would you do about it?
> *Parent.* Go and see the class teacher, have a chat and say 'What can I do to help?'

By putting the focus on assistance to the child they manage to avoid threatening the teacher's self-esteem or challenging the power of the school.

Having established oneself as a non-critical helper through personal contact and diplomatic behaviour a mutual contract between parent and teacher is then subtly negotiated.

> *Interviewer.* What sort of things do you talk about?
>
> *Parent.* Well mainly Jeanne's reading which I had to . . . I'd brought up . . . I mean, she knew my concern, and she'll sort of say 'Jeanne's done that reading; coming on, do you agree?' Or I'll say 'Jeanne's read last night to me, I'm pleased yes . . .' general, nothing particularly intense, but just sort of let her know that, well she knows I'm interested. She just sort of keeps me in touch.

Of course whether the co-operation from the school (through discussion, lending schemes and books, etc.) is given because these parents are fellow-professionals (which they do not hide), is an open question. Do schools trust them to be capable of providing suitable help? Do teachers support such help through fear of alienating them? It is likely that another boundary between home and school is defined by the school's perception of the parents' capacities to give educative help to their children. As a non-professional parent described earlier: 'I did once ask if there was any way I could do anything for Jenny at home . . . they found it better if we just left it to them.' As we shall show, however, in the next chapter, there are many unrecognised ways in which parents of all backgrounds perform an educative role.

Acting to get things done

In direct contrast to the teacher-parents who are willing to accept the way things are, others demonstrate through their talk a sense of purposeful action and a willingness to question the school immediately they feel the need for information or intervention. They do not hesitate to 'pick up the phone', or 'write a very angry letter', 'go up to the school and complain about it fairly bitterly'. They monitor carefully and systematically their children's experience of schooling through checking homework and questioning and observing their children. Unlike those who feel constrained by shared professionalism, these parents are well aware of the benefits of professional knowledge and the advantage they feel it gives them compared to other parents.

One parent who had trained as a mature student certainly found she changed her approach to teachers:

> As a new parent, before I went into teaching, I had the feeling 'they know all about it', there's an *aura* about teaching and, you know, er a gap, but then once I'd gone to the college of education, I jut sort of felt 'well, they're just ordinary people, trained to do the job' and I had every *right* to say 'well, how is he coming on' and 'why is there so little in his book?' and 'Isn't his spelling awful?' and 'What do you do about handwriting, you know, it was barely legible.' That *type* of question, and far more confident to ask this.

These parents, while primarily concerned with their own children, are also prepared to take action on behalf of all children. One gave his views on segregated craft for boys and girls and described exactly how he was going to complain formally to the school, the governors and the area office, (an example of the useful knowledge of the education system referred to earlier). Another explained how she had criticised the size of the tutor group in the sixth form, with a successful outcome.

A marked feature with these parents is the importance attached to gathering *evidence* with which to support their actions. 'Getting the facts' is seen as necessary partly as a strategy to prevent being fobbed off with 'platitudes and clichés', partly to prevent accusations of simply being an over-anxious parent, and partly to demonstrate their professionalism in being 'objective' rather than relying on gossip, hearsay or the child's words. Intervention is therefore not hasty or ill-thought-out but prepared for in advance with arguments marshalled and strategies planned. These can range from the relatively simple level of preparing questions in advance of parents' evenings to quite detailed gathering of data before going to school. The English teacher's actions over her daughter's 'O' level work is one illustration of this.

These parents are quite aware of the way professionals create distance by hiding behind desks, report cards and work books, and interrupt such behaviour:

> I think I came out quite strongly that I wasn't going to be fooled

by him. And as he started flicking the pages in the report, I said 'there's no need for you to do that because I've prepared it for you so you can just compare the three reports and you'll see what I mean.'

Viewed from the perspective of the school we suspect that these parents are the ones most likely to be regarded as 'interfering' or even 'dangerous enemies'. However, the parents themselves felt they had been successful in most of their dealings with schools and they certainly had no fears that their child would be victimised as a result of their actions. They believe they do have some power to affect their child's experience of schooling and indeed to bring about change in school policy. Solutions to difficulties lie in getting the evidence, preparing the argument and taking immediate action. Rather than seeing a change of school as a solution, they put their trust in intervention to change the school. However, rather than allowing the school to define the boundaries, the sense of personal power they possess enables these parents to determine the kind of relationship between home and school that they want and to get it. Their talk suggests that this is true for many aspects of their lives and that their shared professionalism with schools only gives a sharper edge to getting things done there.

Treading a fine line

More evidence on the way boundaries between home and school are perceived comes from a group of teacher-parents who, although not inhibited by their status, nevertheless are aware of it to the extent that they assess what is appropriate behaviour for a parent from a teacher's perspective. As a result they feel they have to tread a fine line, always balancing their rights as parents with what they see as the rights of schools to manage their own affairs. As parents, they will intervene in aspects that concern their child's security or happiness, such as bullying or adjustment to school, but not in what are regarded as internal matters such as the curriculum or school policy on home/school relations.

Let's say I think *such* a situation [an open day with a five-minute appointment] is of very limited value, in spite of that nevertheless to me it is their own professional decision . . . and therefore I, as I have no standing in the school other than that of a parent, erm, I try, I would tend to restrict anything I have to say to the school to my own child. I think it would be wrong of me to suggest how they should run their school which would include parents' evenings.

But provided the area of concern is perceived as legitimately that of a parent, they will visit school, ask questions, and raise problems.

Awareness of role boundaries also affects their actions at home. One parent, describing his decision not to teach his child to read, explained, 'I've always felt professionally that that *particular* area should be left up to the school, so that the parents should play a supportive role and not the other way round.' Professional knowledge is however used to make judgements about their children's progress, and knowledge and understanding of children in general informs observations of their own children. Confidence in their own professional judgement also influences their contact with schools.

> When my daughter had just started the comprehensive school and we were invited, I think the wording on the invitation was 'If you have any particular problems, or if your child has any particular problems, then we'd be pleased to see you.' We found Jane has settled, *we think*, with comprehensive life, so we didn't bother to go.

For other parents, the judgement as to whether there were problems or not might have been more difficult to determine. We have certainly found that schools that define a boundary through invitations to 'come and see us if you have any problems' create a feeling of exclusion amongst parents whose children are progressing well and also create problems for parents who cannot decide whether their problem is a legitimate one in the school's eyes!

By continually using this professional perspective, however, these teacher-parents can find themselves experiencing tension when their own professional judgements collide with those of the school.

> There was quite an extensive list of the preparation work that we as parents should be doing and I must say my hackles rose . . . and I didn't do it . . . partly because it's not the sort of thing I would expect children to do myself before they start school.

This acute awareness of the boundaries, however, leaves these parents in a difficult position if problems remain unresolved. While those who are loathe to intervene at all see the only solution as a change of school, they regard this as the final answer when other strategies have failed.

> I suppose you might say if communication broke down to *that* extent, the only thing we feel we can reasonably do as parents, in as much as parents I don't feel we can tell the school how they must run it, how they should, er, structure their learning situation, therefore I suppose, we as parents, the only thing we can do would be to withdraw Stuart from it.

This group of teacher-parents seem to epitomise most the schizophrenia of being in the two roles, and the underlying tension of the lay/professional relationship. Those who maintain a low profile or accept the way things are avoid open conflict and in this way attempt to minimise the tension. Those who take action to get things done through the gathering of data and evidence establish power and the comfort of feeling secure in their parental rights. By taking neither of these stances but attempting to tread the fine line, these parents find it most difficult to negotiate a satisfactory relationship with schools.

BOUNDARIES: NOT FIXED BUT DYNAMIC

Becoming parents themselves opens teachers' eyes to the variety of ways in which the lay/professional relationship creates barriers between home and school. As we have seen, how they deal with these barriers varies considerably and this must challenge the view that middle-class parents find relationships with schools unproblematic. What seems to be at the heart of the problem is the nature of the power that schools are perceived to have and the degree to which parents feel able to challenge that power. Becoming a parent helps teachers to understand more the vulnerability experienced when one's child or one's self is going to be judged by others, the feelings engendered by encounters with authority figures, the helplessness of an individual faced with a complex system. They begin to realise the many ways in which policies and practices they took for granted exclude parents from being really involved in their children's education.

I'm much more aware of the ways in which schools tend to fob parents off with the platitudes and clichés, and again much more guilty about the way in which I myself fall into it.

They begin to question the nature of communication and contact, in particular its generalised nature, and whether reports and parents' evenings are adequate ways of keeping a check on children's progress, understanding what is happening in schools, and enabling them to be involved. Our study of familiar parents in Chapter 5 showed how closer contact and involvement with schools led many of them to identify more with the school's goals and activities. Similarly the experience of parenting helps teachers to understand and identify more with the parental perspective on schools. The theme of this book is 'listening to parents'; perhaps a good place for teachers to start is with their own colleagues who have children!

Boundaries of many kinds exist between home and school. What we hope this account has shown is that far from being able to define these with any certainty they are created and sustained in different ways for different parents. Class, race and gender all play a part in this process but equally important are the perceptions parents and teachers have of their own and each other's role and the way these influence the kind of relationship between them. The nature of the boundaries will change with closer contact between the family and the school and shifts in the balance of power between the two. As long as parents choose, though, to have their children educated at school rather than 'or otherwise', boundaries of some kind will exist; the process of defining these is not just a matter of legislation and formal structures but also negotiated in the dynamics of interactions between individual parents and teachers.

7

Parents as Educators

It is a common experience for teachers to be asked by parents what those parents can do to help their children learn. The nature of the communication which takes place between teachers and parents in this area is problematic, and both parties express dissatisfaction at its outcomes. Teachers may fear that parents are going to become 'interfering' or else, with the best of intentions, initiate damaging patterns which they, the teachers, then have to put right, whilst parents may feel loathe to ask for advice for fear of 'treading on teachers' toes', or else come to see any attempt at 'partnership' in this area as an empty exercise:

> You go along to the school, and he sits and reiterates platitudes to you, and you make the same obeisance. It's rather like going to church you know, paternosters and throwing holy water around, and touch the prayer book as you go out of the door. He feels relieved because he's seen the parents, but he couldn't probably care less what I think.

Certainly, responses to requests from parents for advice about helping seem to consist as often of what *not* to do, as of suggestions about possible positive actions: 'we certainly tell them, don't sit with a book and er, say, this says 'the' and er, try to teach them to read in that way.' And what seems to be rare indeed is for teachers to solicit information from parents about how best to help the child:

> *Father.* We have a problem 'cos he's diabetic . . .
> *Teacher.* Yes, I realise that . . . the only thing we haven't had is an information pamphlet which says how to deal with a diabetic child in school.

Mother. I gave the Headmaster one . . . but I can get you another
   one if you like.
Teacher. I would, please, because I think it is very important . . .
   I'd much rather be in a situation where I knew what was
   happening . . . I'm not so sure that I would know exactly what
   to do if . . .
Mother. . . . just that if he sort of says that he feels funny, then
   he gradually goes down and down until he can't be bothered
   to do anything. If he gets that far, which he doesn't normally,
   just give him something with sugar in . . . like a drink of milk
   . . . a teaspoon of sugar in water or something like that, you
   know.
   [*Discussion about insulin, carrying boiled sweets, wearing a
   necklet with a telephone number on it.*]
Teacher. Thanks very much. That's been useful.

What characterised this particular consultation interview was a
genuine exchange of information. After the discussion about the
boy's diabetes, the mother goes on to initiate a discussion of a topic
the teacher has been doing with the class on 'life in Georgian times';
she tells him how taken her son was with this, and how he told all
about it at home — a sure sign his interest has been engaged. The
teacher takes the opportunity to explain something of his methods
and what he hopes the children will learn:

Teacher. What I try do is . . . to give them some information, but
   not all of it. I say, 'I'll tell you a bit about how people enjoyed
   themselves during Georgian times. . . fist fighting was very
   popular. Now, nowadays, if they have a world heavyweight
   championship, it goes for fifteen rounds . . . you'd be
   surprised to find out how long they used to fight for in
   Georgian times.' And then of course they want me to tell
   them, but I won't. They've got to use the reference material
   to find that out, and then they'll come — 'Oh look they used
   to fight fifty, sixty rounds.' Well, I mean, it's gone in you see,
   and it means more to them because, if you like, you've tickled
   their fancy, and then they've gone away and . . . because
   being able to find information for themselves is important . . .
Mother. They went to work when I were at that age, then! — he
   found that fascinating.
   [*Discussion about the factory children.*]
Teacher. Next half term, all being well, we shall be using the

population census returns for Nuthall, 1841, 51, 61, 70, and building up family pictures of what it was like in Victorian times, and then trying to compare that with their own family situation, so I hope he enjoys that.

Mother. Yeah, he seems happy up to now, anyway. Thank you.

Father. Thank you very much.

The meeting has been quoted so extensively because it is in such marked contrast to the earlier father's description of reciprocal platitudes, the performing of a duty, etc., and would seem to illuminate the potential for such exchanges of information to enhance both teachers' and parents' knowledge, skills and abilities to help children learn. In the context of parents helping their children, we have come across very few examples of teachers asking parents about the kinds of things they already do to enhance their children's learning.

Where this does more noticeably occur is at the pre-school stage, in settings like the Sheffield Institute of Education's Home Visiting Scheme, where in 1979 ways were sought to support and sustain the families of pre-school children by recognising and extending family skills, through the communicating of approval of what they were already attempting. Similar initiatives have taken place in Birmingham, Coventry, Nottingham and Liverpool, and rest on the assumption that parents have to be 'worked with, not compensated for'.

This recognition of parental knowledge, skills and expertise in the learning process of their children often requires an initial act of faith, since if you ask parents directly what they do as 'educators' of their children, they may themselves declare that they don't! When they go on to talk about their activities, conversations and relationships with their children, however, it becomes clear that far from doing nothing, they may simply be unaware of the significance of what they *are* doing for their children's learning. Their roles as 'educators' do not consist of carefully thought-out, planned, organised activities, but form part of the rhythm of 'family life'. What parents do consciously, is to 'parent', often without recognising the 'educational' component and potential of the relationship between parents and children:

But I don't think you ever think, it, it must be educational to a degree . . . I don't think you ever set a time of day aside and think, 'Right, we'll do some clever stuff!' you know.

If parents are not always themselves aware of what they know and do, then 'listening to parents' becomes an invaluable way of uncovering and building upon the skills and expertise they do possess.

PARENTS' CONCEPTS ABOUT LEARNING AND TEACHING

Teachers themselves may well be hard-pressed if asked to articulate the theories they operate in the teaching and learning process, so it is hardly surprising that parents do not readily do so. Listening to parents give accounts of family life, however, and learning how to ask the right questions to promote such dialogue, does uncover a number of operational concepts which they employ in dealing with their children.

Of course, parents have a more intimate knowledge of their own children than teachers can ever hope to have, and it is this intimacy which develops in all the different settings of family life, and as the child changes, develops, and matures, that enables parents to develop the skills to motivate each child in a different way:

But then again, I suppose different children would react in different ways, but I think you get to know your child, or your children, and know in exactly what way you can sort of, make them even more interested — because a remark I could say to Chris, if I'd said the same remark to Andrew, it would've p'raps shut him off.

Parents observe what their children enjoy doing, and they make judgements about why this is so:

I think he's got a natural talent for copying things. I mean, he sits, and he'll draw . . . and he copies really well. He's got the patience, and I think he gets a lot of satisfaction out of being able to do things like that, and I think he likes technical drawing because a lot of it is reproduction, and it seems to appeal to him.

In comparing their children, parents pick out basic personality traits:

Mother. He just takes it all in his stride, doesn't he?
Father. Yeah, he's very easy-going, for a start, and he just goes and gets on with it and that's it.

87

Mother. Which is nice.

Father. Yeah, whereas Alan I think, might be a little bit different. Well, it's chalk and cheese really, isn't it? John's easy-going, and Alan's all hustle-and-bustle.

They may feel that aspects of their children's personalities pose a problem, and seek to intervene to improve matters:

Melanie's got one failing: she loves to get involved in things — temporarily. After a few weeks, the newness wears off and she loses interest. We've had this with horse-riding . . . recorder . . . drama . . . anyway I put my foot down, and I said, 'You've got to see something through.' Anyway, she went into the Guides, and she's quite happy . . . all right, we've had to give her a push, you know, before she joined, but that's typical of her.

Parents certainly develop a repertoire of skills for handling each of their children, and learn what 'works' with them, and what doesn't:

She used to bring books home from school, and we used to lie down on the rug together, and I'd help her with her reading. It got that bad that I was getting annoyed, which is very unusual, and in the end, she just wouldn't do it. She knew it, but she wouldn't do it. And in the end, I threw the book, you know, 'Sod it! I've had enough!' — and virtually straight after, she never looked back. That's the way that's worked with Yvonne. The same with swimming. She could do it, but she was giggling and laughing, and wouldn't concentrate, so I said, 'Right, sod off in the little pool with the babies. I don't want to know. I'm not wasting any more time on you.' And she went in the little pool for a while, had a little cry, and then came back, and off she went!

There is no formal training for this aspect of parenting. They are abilities which parents, through this intimate, day-to-day contact with their children, learn 'on the job'.

It is perhaps not surprising that parents also have recourse to heredity as a possible explanation for their children's abilities or lack of them:

It's easy to blame heredity, but we've gone back through three or four generations, and there hasn't been a decent writer on my side, a male . . . and he has practised . . . the teacher at the junior school lent him some of his *own* books on handwriting, and he did practise . . . so it's not a matter of taking the easy way out and blaming his ancestors.

Parents are also aware of modelling as a component of learning — 'They'd seen us reading. They knew that erm, there was a lot to be got out of reading' — and they also make a link between their children's interests and abilities and their own:

You used to take them to see me play football and volleyball — 'You teach *me* to play that, Dad! Oh, I hope I can do it. I'm gonna be one of them when I grow up', you know, like all little boys are.

Parents' awareness of themselves as a model may be provoked unexpectedly when they clearly recognise their child's not necessarily-attractive behaviour as their own:

It's just like looking at myself really. She's very stubborn. No, not really stubborn . . . quite self-willed, shall we say, and so am I, so basically I suppose, I know roughly what she's going to do, because she reacts very much the same as I do to things; . . . sometimes when you watch them playing, you can see yourself . . . and you think, 'Oh, do I do that? Oh, I don't say that!' and I suppose you do — they just mimic really, don't they? — dreadful thought!

Children are not, thankfully, faithful reproductions of their parents, despite the 'chip off the old block' element parents often describe, and they do display abilities all their own. Whilst recognising such innate ability, parents also observe that their children will learn better if they are really interested, and as well as the 'push' mentioned earlier, or the clear indication that father has come to the end of his patience, some kind of incentive or reward is also seen as an appropriate tool:

He used to moan like buggery about this French, and we went down to school . . . and we had a word with his French teacher, and we put it to him that in our opinion he wasn't being given enough incentive, a big enough carrot, and the French teacher said that in a while, they were going to be segregated, and those

89

that were catching on very quickly would be put together — and this worked . . . Because every time he goes, he's given something to do, a target to aim for, and he'll go for it.

Learning is seen then, as being promoted by this mixture of innate ability, modelling, conscious or otherwise, and motivation, which might need a 'push' or a 'pull'. On top of all this, as competition for the instrumental rewards of learning gets tougher, children must increase their effort and consciously apply themselves in order to capitalise upon their own abilities:

I'd like him to take 'A' levels. If he applies himself, I think he's clever enough to do it. I think he realises himself that er, opportunities being what they are, if you're gonna make something of yourself, it's becoming more and more essential that you *do* stay on.

Teachers can develop the skill when listening to parents to recognise the concepts parents are employing, even if they do not necessarily use the same vocabulary (modelling, motivation, etc.) to describe the process they are engaged in. Such concepts do not appear to be too dissimilar to those which teachers operate in the classroom. What parents *do* have available to them is a greater degree of flexibility to act in a *responsive* rather than a *directive* way. They can follow their children's leads without undue pressure to sustain an activity beyond the child's own interest:

I taught him to read because he wanted to read, and he got on well, but then the summer came, and then that was it, he wanted to go out and play, which is the way. He's only four, let him go.

This pattern of learning is one which is much more characteristic of the home than of the school.

THE HOME AS A LEARNING ENVIRONMENT

Perhaps it is their awareness of the differences between the two worlds of home and school which causes parents to devalue the contribution they themselves make to their children's learning. We have seen earlier the formation of the idea that 'proper' learning begins with entry into formal schooling. And from this very early point parents observe from their children's behaviour that they too experience home and school as two very different places, with different expectations operating:

> When Chris started school, he came home one day and walked out of his coat and dropped it just where it was, behind him, you see. So I said, 'Chris, pick up your coat for me, will you love please?' And he just wanders by. I could've been speaking in Swahili. So I said to him. 'Chris?' — '(sigh) Yes mum?' — I says, 'Will you pick your coat up, please' — 'In a minute' . . . I thought I'll tell him once, I'll tell him twice, but ooh it hurts to tell him again. So I got cross then, and I says to him, 'When your teacher asks you to do anything, d'you tell her you'll do it in a minute?' He says, 'N-o-oh!' I says, 'Well, do you ignore her then?' — 'N-o-o-oh'. So I says, 'Well, why can't you be a good boy for me?' And he says, 'Mum, when I come home, all my good's worn out' . . . He'd been so good that he just couldn't last any longer . . . and he'll switch it on again at nine o'clock tomorrow morning! . . . of course, we finished up laughing about it. *I* picked his coat up!

The degree of egocentricity afforded to the child is one of the characteristics of the home, and it is seen as appropriate by many parents that it is this way round:

> I think children have got two personalities, haven't they? At home here with me . . . let's put it this way . . . if he's a rascal, he's a rascal here . . . I personally think it's the right way round . . . you know, his roguishness comes out at home . . . at least this is the impression we've got from these Parents' Evenings . . . that he's very quiet, you'd hardly know he was there. And yet at home, it's a bit like a whirlwind sometimes.

As they become older, children may become more conscious of the differing constraints, and actively manage the impressions they create:

> *Father*. When we go up to school, it's almost certainly confirmed that, you know she is no sluggard, she works, she enjoys her work. Erm, basically the teachers are pleased with her. They always have been so far.
> *Mother*. At home, she tends to act as though she's stupid, don't she?

Where children's behaviour is markedly different at home and at school, tapping into parental perspectives may provide teachers with some valuable insights.

The egocentricity which is allowed, the flexibility, and the space and time available for responsiveness in the home, means that the learning which takes place there is not a one-way process. Parents, although older and more experienced than their children, continue to learn from their children as they enter new parental roles. And in times of fairly rapid social change, the experience of children differs so markedly from that of their parents, that the parents become in a sense immigrants to a new world, and must learn from their children about how to live in that world. Parents learn about children, about child development and its trends, about new ways of teaching and learning, about strategies of schooling, about the variety of behaviour and experience to which their children's associates will expose them. In this sense, contact with the life of a child opens up a new vision of the world, and the full range of the child's activities becomes a potential source of education for the parent. The experience of adjustment and readjustment to changes in the child, given the child's comparatively rapid rate of matura-tion, is another potential source of education for the parent, so that interaction with the child inevitably requires continuous shifts on the part of the parent and serves as a pressure for continuous learning.

The shared learning which takes place within the family is not, of course, confined to parents and children, but also takes place between brothers and sisters. They serve not only as role models for each other but also as sources of evaluation, as challengers, and as stimulators. They may also have direct educational influence on each other, although the ways in which such education proceeds are so much a part of the fabric of daily existence that they are sometimes difficult to discern:

He's shown Yvonne . . . I'm thinking of one particular event . . . an anniversary . . . they came up one morning giggling, and we could hear pots rattling upstairs and er, giggles, as they spilled the tea, that sort of thing, and they brought a tray with two breakfasts on, and David has set to and started it, and we've had continuing reports: the first time Yvonne turned the bacon over . . . the second time she did an egg and er, little things like that as he's gradually helped her along . . . or she's poured the tea out, something like that. Oh, it's lovely.

Parents of course, receive no professional training for their task, and must simply learn 'on the job'. In a similar way to teachers, however, they are subjected to a sometimes confusing mixture of influences, fashions, advice, expectations and admonishments. A parallel trend in both activities has been a gradual move towards 'child-centredness' — a move from a largely authoritarian to a largely democratic model, the essence of which is a principle of reciprocity. Children are taught to respect the rights and wishes of others, via endless verbal persuasion and reiteration. It is a painfully slow process, dependent on the gradual growth of self-awareness and social empathy. The child is valued as a person whose wishes and desires must be respected, and they are accorded status in their own right as they learn to accord it to others:

> We explain why, in *our* opinion, why we don't think they should have it, or do it. Now, if they've got a constructive argument why they should, we're quite willing to be persuaded otherwise. It's a discussion format that we use. We discuss virtually everything as a family unit. It's not just mum and dad deciding, and not necessarily the kids deciding.

It is often in this democratic context that much of the talk between parents and children takes place, characterised, as mentioned earlier, by a responsiveness to the child's interests, a negotiation of meaning, an encouragement to put current activities into a wider context of consequences, feelings and principles.

Most of the conversations in the home are initiated by the child, arise spontaneously from the activity in hand, and are free from any pressure to teach and learn particular skills and facts. The learning that does take place at home usually occurs via interaction with the adult as participant. It is idiosyncratic and personal, it can be short-burst or obsessively sustained for long periods, depending on the child's own interest and the rhythms of family life. Demands such as shopping can simply be a temporary break before an activity is lovingly resumed, and the contexts and environments for learning range from the house, the garden, the street, to the car park, shops, waste-ground, neighbours, shopkeeper, milkman.

All of this forms a sharp contrast with many features of school-based learning, where talk is predominantly initiated by the teacher, who often asks questions to which she already knows the answer, where the environment is largely confined to the classroom, and where what is learned is short-burst, fragmented, and compacted into segments of time. A little of something every day seems to be the recipe, regardless of stage of development, particular needs, or patterns of interest or skill at the time. As one bright, lively child commented to her mother at an Open Evening: 'This is my interest book, mummy. I hate doing my interest book.'

Parents too, by virtue of their own biography and life-positions, provide a source of contact with the contemporary world. Here, a working father describes his five-year old twin sons' interest in his job as foreman in a lace factory:

> They ask me what I do, and how's lace made, and what's it made from, and how does it make it, and why does it come out like that, and what happens to it when it does come out like that?

And parents quickly become a source of history!

> We didn't have nursery facilities or anything, and try to explain *that* to Jenny! She often asks what *I* used to do at nursery, and . . . 'Did you used to do this at your party?' You try and explain to Jenny that it was a novelty for anybody to have a party. I mean, we didn't get the things that they get now, and she says, 'Why not? . . . well, they don't cost much.' — So *she* says!

Use is also made of relatives, or friends in the neighbourhood, who either have some 'inside knowledge' of the educational system *per se*, or who have skills or knowledge which the family itself does not possess, but which can be tapped into on a mutual basis:

> *Mother.* . . . if we can't help with the schoolwork . . . we go and ask somebody who can, like with erm, fractions. I was never any good at them at school, and er, the chap next-door-but-one is a woodworker, you know, and he deals with fractions, so we nip round to him. We always find someone to help, and we've got dictionaries upstairs, er, encyclopaedias, and we get them down.
>
> *Father.* It works both ways. We've had kiddies coming round here asking us things . . . we've finished up with three or four encyclopaedias stretched across the settee helping David's friend with her homework . . . there are one or two more parents that think the same as us, you know, they'll say, 'Go and ask Joe and Nancy' — just as we would say, 'Go and ask Jeff', to help them with their homework.

And grandparents, as well as supplying additional variety of experience, traditionally supply additional freedom:

> They seem to have a lot of fun with their grandparents . . . because they're allowed to do what they like when we're not there . . . and me dad's got a garage which they can go in, and they've got their toy cars in there. They jack up and play underneath them and pretend that they're doing the same as mechanics!

So, the curriculum of the home, and parents' roles as educators within it, are not carefully thought out, planned, organised, but are part of the rhythm of family life. When asked to articulate their own contribution to the process, parents do so in terms of taking an interest, offering support, validating and confirming children's abilities and interests, becoming involved:

> I think a lot of parents do it without realising that you're doing it. Just the fact that you show interest in what they're doing, and erm, you know, sort of, become involved. Not to take over. I think it's important that you don't take over . . . I think you've just got to be available.

'Being available' is of course not always easy for the teacher with responsibility for perhaps 30 children, and the difficulties she may face are illustrated by this conversation at a Parents' Evening:

> *Mother.* He'll say, 'Oh, I haven't finished any writing yet. It's taken me a long time today 'cos I keep queuing up.' This queuing up! I think he gets a bit frustrated sometimes . . .
> *Teacher.* Yes, it must be, really, for them . . . we're actually trying to work on this, to reduce the number of children in that area, but of course then it means there's an awful lot of children not done any writing . . . we're not satisfied
> *Mother.* No, it's not very good, 'cos they're just waiting and queuing. I know one day I said, 'What have you been doing this afternoon?' and he says, 'Nothing', and I says why, and he says, 'I've been sitting at the table just waiting for the teacher to come to me. I kept putting me hand up, but she was busy.'

One can sympathise here with the bored and frustrated child, the dissatisfied mother and the hard-pressed teacher. We would not advocate that schools should simply imitate the 'good home' even if that could be defined. Although they both have an educative function, the school complements the informality of the home by necessarily introducing the child to more formal ways of acquiring and utilising knowledge, and to a way of life which enables the child to adjust his or her own needs to those of others. The organisation of the school draws in this task upon the skills of trained professionals, and what is suggested is that these professional teachers can, in recognising the learning environment provided by the home, utilise the resources it offers in ways which turn upon its head the more traditional notion of providing compensation for its inadequacies.

EDUCATIVE STRATEGIES USED BY PARENTS

We have seen how parents *do* operate concepts of teaching and learning; we have heard how they observe their children, evaluate and assess their behaviour, and how they respond and intervene in the learning process, developing and honing their skills in the routinised but changing patterns of family life.

Although they may not describe themselves as educators, or see what they do as an organised activity, the strategies they use to help their children learn can be conceived of as forming a systematic pattern: observation — evaluation — intervention. This pattern can be seen in operation in relation to materials sent to parents of pre-school children, designed to practice various pre-reading skills such as shape-recognition, hand-eye co-ordination, working from left to right, etc:

Mother. The folder gave us ideas, didn't it?

Father. It did, 'cos we didn't stick to the folder. We did the colouring. Well, he did the colouring, and then when we seen what a mess he made of that, we said that's it. We left it, and went on to these, and when he'd done them, well, we just asked him to er, which two's the same, and he did them all right. We didn't go on to those. We stopped with these, then his letters, just to get him to hold a pencil, you know, and once he could control the pencil, it'd come even better then. But such as crayoning — any old how! Well, it's a matter of holding your pencil then, and trying . . . once you can control your pencil or your crayon, then I think it'll come easier. So we did two or three of the exercises, and then we went on us own. We carried on on us own. We didn't bother then with the folder.

Mother. But it gave you ideas. You wouldn't have thought of some of them what we did, if we hadn't have got the folder to start with.

These parents observed their son's performance with the materials, assessed his ability to use a pencil, intervened to try to remedy his difficulty, and abandoned those activities in which he was failing in favour of helping him towards more initial success. They adapted the materials to suit their son's particular needs, and went on to develop the ideas they got from the folder. If such strategies are already familiar to parents, the potential for providing materials or ideas for learning, to which parents can apply the intimate knowledge they possess of how to get the best out of their children, becomes obvious. What would be required in making such provision in response to parental requests of how they can help their children, would be to uncover for them the positive things they already do — often without knowing it — to confirm and validate their own good practice, in the same way as these parents do for their children, and to build upon and extend such practice. Just as the father ignored and abandoned his son's unsuccessful crayoning and concentrated on developing his successes, teachers might abandon telling parents what *not* to do, in favour of recognising and utilising the educative strategies they unconsciously do use.

When parents intervene more consciously, it is often to promote the child's ability to organise her life and learning more effectively:

It's not that we think that she's got to do the homework, or perhaps there's an element of that. But it's more the er, she's so upset herself when it gets to the Monday morning or when it gets to, you know, eight o'clock or half past eight on Sunday night, if she remembers that she hasn't done it, you know, the panic, and the worry — so we tend to get on at her beforehand.

Engaging with the child in the process of organising materials, activities, space, or time, may also be initiated by the child:

Within a couple of days he was sitting here: 'I wonder which to do first tomorrow mum?' So I said, 'Why? What have you got to do?' — 'I've got topic work to do, I've got number work to do,

I've got reading to do', and he liked topic the very best, so every
single day we had it at tea-time and then again at breakfast. It was
a toss-up whether he did topic first as that was his favourite, or
whether he got his other, erm, jobs out of the way to leave topic
till the end.

Such organising skills, which parents are in an ideal position to
promote, are exactly those which are required to cope with the way
learning is patterned in schools. When the child starts school, the
'curriculum of the home' is inevitably influenced by the curriculum
of the school. Parents will have certain expectations of the school
and of the ways in which it will benefit the child. These expectations
will be added to and amended by the child herself as she 'brings the
school into the home' in her accounts and in her observable
behaviour, and by the contacts and communications the parents
begin to have with the school and the teachers directly.

As they continue to observe and assess their children's learning,
in the ways we have seen, parents' own intervention may become
increasingly conscious, as their children become 'pupils' and as they
become the parents of pupils. As the child enters formal schooling,
parents become more aware of activities which might be interpreted
as supportive of the kinds of learnings which the child will encounter
in school. In making judgements about their child's experience of
schooling, they may promote and complement this experience, or
they may take action to compensate for perceived failing in the
school curriculum, the ultimate example of this being to remove the
child from the school. Other parents at this end of the scale undertake covert teaching themselves, or hire a tutor for extra tuition in
problematic areas.

PARENTS AS EDUCATORS: A TYPOLOGY

Figure 7.1 represents the over-arching influences on parents'
educative roles and offers a typology of those roles in relation to the
child's schooling. 'Parents as educators' is not a static concept; an
attempt has been made to demonstrate how parents perform their
role as part of the dynamics of family life. The family has a life-
span, and the roles of parents acting as educators will develop and
change as the lives of its members are lived. In addition, the child
himself asserts his individuality and uniqueness, and thereby
influences the contribution parents make to his learning as they

Table 7.1: Parents as educators: a typology

←——————————————————————————→

The active role of the child in the process

Complementary Attitudes, relationships and activities, initiated by parents or children, which by their nature are likely to promote learning — the 'hidden curriculum of the home'.	*Confirmatory* Actively encouraging, supporting, and confirming the work undertaken by the school.	*Compensatory* Parent-initiated action to encourage the school to meet a requirement in which it is perceived to be failing; undertaking the task oneself; supplying alternative personnel to do so.
Socialisation, pre-school experience, preparation for school.	(a) *Home-based* 'Bringing the school into the home', i.e. school-based learning shared.	Supplying the school with information about the child; 'alerting' the school.
Modelling specific skills, attitudes, and behaviour	Homework: attitude to, help with	Undertaking home 'teaching'.
Developing traits conducive to learning, growth, development. 'Moulding'. Regulating the child's handling of materials in space, or activities in time.	(b) *School-based* — parents in the school — parents in the classroom	Hiring a tutor. Removing child to another school.
Outings and activities — providing experiences, resources, mediating the world to the child.	(c) *Linking* (a) and (b) are teacher-parent contacts and communications — how they affect the parent-as-educator roles — the 'making of home/school relations'.	
Having aspirations and expectations.		
Careers guidance.		

The changing nature of parental educative roles

←——————————————————————————→

Over time-span of the family life-cycle

follow his leads and are constrained by his personality.

In recognising 'parents as educators', the role of the professional teacher becomes that of co-educator. In a genuine partnership between teachers and parents, the teacher complements the parents' unique specialist knowledge of their child with the professional's wider knowledge of the current theories on child development. Parental strategies developed in all the various settings of family life can be encouraged with access to materials and ideas to enable such strategies to be effectively utilised. Parents' skills and opportunities in the informal learning environment of the home, and the tolerance afforded to the child's idiosyncracies, develop alongside the professional's introduction to the more structured, institutionalised setting of the school, which prepares the child for the institutional constraints he will encounter throughout life. It becomes part of the teacher's role to discover kinds of learning other than the already familiar school-based kinds, and to enable parents to discover and develop the contribution they make to the process. With encouragement and active listening from the teacher, parents can describe practices and approaches which many teachers would admire and applaud. For teachers who wish to work towards a more genuine partnership in home/school relations, recognising, encouraging, and enabling parents-as-educators can be the beginning of creating different but complementary roles in the educational process.

Part Three

Working with Parents: The Development
of Effective Practice

8

Strategies for Developing a
Home/School Programme

In Part Two of this book we have given considerable emphasis to the examination of parental perspectives and experience, as they are expressed in four overlapping accounts of parents' dealings with their children's schools. We have adjusted the focus to show this experience in different lights and from different angles, so as to expose the differences of background, attitude and experience that will exist in any cross-section of parents. Above all, we have provided an extended opportunity for readers to listen to the voices of real parents in a form that is not available in the hurly-burly of everyday life in our schools. Listening to parents, in our view, provides access to knowledge and understanding that cannot be gained in any other way and which is of immense practical value.

In Part Three we are concerned to identify strategies through which schools and teachers can find ways of listening to parents for themselves and to tease out the implications of this for the development of more effective home/school practice. In this chapter there is consideration of some of the strategic issues and problems that are involved. 'Listening to parents' is considered as a key element in a school's overall philosophy and an important influence upon its ways of working; it can be a key tool in the planning and evaluation of home/school activity and, above all, a rich source of ideas for the improvement of existing practice and the development of new forms. This is followed in Chapter 9 by a detailed consideration of the practical arrangements that such a strategy calls for, together with a range of illustrations, examples and suggestions which are felt to be useful to hard-pressed teachers who wish to improve their work.

The need for a school-based approach

Growing experience in this and other areas (such as curriculum development) suggest that it is at the *institutional* level of the individual school that development and change are most likely to be effectively realised — or fail to get off the ground. For this is the critical point in the operationalising of new ideas and practice, where teachers, pupils and parents meet and interact. It is in individual schools where the education service stands the best chance of becoming aware of, and responding to, the needs and experience of those children and families for whom it is provided: it cannot be achieved by general formulae and bland prescription.

Schools *are* different, in home/school matters as elsewhere. There are crucially important differences in the character and organisation of neigbourhoods which are highly significant for parents and families and which have implications for the education of their children. This is true, whether schools recognise it or not. So the individual school, in important ways, offers the most effective focal point for the organisation of home/school effort and for the development of effective practice. For it is mainly through the interaction of individuals that the needs and wishes of parents, in all their complexity, can be acknowledged, appropriate responses planned and practical initiatives attempted.

That is not to deny, however, the importance of both a wider view and a role for the education service as a whole. In the first place, many schools suffer from a narrowness of perspective and vision; the other side of familiarity can be parochialism or tunnel vision. So there can be an important role to be played, for example, by a home/school liaison teacher scheme, in bringing in a picture of the outside world and providing access to other perspectives and experience, or in acting as a catalyst in the development of thinking and practice.

In the second place, there are many important areas in which individual schools cannot 'go it alone', where wider recognition and action are required, both nationally, via the DES, or locally through local education authority institutions and agencies. Examples include:

- the introduction of enabling legislation and regulation;
- the formulation of general policy, guidance and support;
- the allocation of resources;
- the introduction and support of key initiatives and development work;

- the co-ordination and dissemination of 'good practice';
- the identification of, and provision for, training needs.

Preparing for change

In this chapter 'listening to parents' is explored as a key tool in the planning, organisation and development of home/school relations. However, it cannot exist in a vacuum, but in the context of a range of competing demands upon the energy and attention of both schools and families. New ways of thinking and working make important demands upon existing ways of formulating policy and making decisions.

Here we can identify a number of areas which, sooner or later, will need to be thought through. We do not present these as a series of clear-cut choices between alternatives, but as the need to work out a balance between competing purposes, styles of working and changing areas of priority. Even to begin to listen to parents makes demands on each of these:

The *needs of schools and families*, as we have shown in Part Two, sometimes coincide, sometimes partially overlap, but often differ in important ways. Whilst schools and families (and individuals within them) will 'draw the line' differently, and in different ways, the recognition of both common ground and important differences, has to be acknowledged as a basic element in any home/school strategy.

One consequence of such a view is the matter of how far schools should take the initiative in shaping home/school policy and practice, and how far and in what ways it should be *responsive* to parental perspectives and experience. For, as we have shown, most current home/school activity is really on the school's terms, with parents left to operate at the margins of school life. Problems in this area are likely to emerge or to be reinforced through existing styles of leadership and management, in the ways important decisions are made involving staff and parents and responsibility for doing things is shared. Listening to parents clearly requires a shift towards more open styles of management and the greater participation of parents in the life and work of schools than is often the case. It also calls for thoughtful planning on the one hand and the ability to act spontaneously and take advantage of opportunities as they arise, on the other.

One of the consequences of more 'open' relationships between schools and the families they serve is the need to bring additional aspects of the working relationship into the open for close examination and to arrive at, either formally or through shared understandings, agreement about what is to be done. One school we work with, for example, finds it increasingly useful to distinguish between:

(a) Areas where basic agreement is sought, policy thrashed out through discussion and those procedures which are to be followed by *all* staff agreed. An example here might be the arrangements for parents' evenings, which concern *all* teachers and parents, albeit at different times.

(b) Other areas, often areas of growth and professional development, where involvement is felt to be more appropriately voluntary, where participation is deliberately limited and small-scale, with experience being fed into the wider scene in a constructively critical way. An example here might be home visiting schemes, about which teachers and parents have a range of views.

In educational contexts, such a distinction might be characteristically thought of as different *basic* activities and *further development*. A basic programme would be concerned with widely held values and practices, or those which provide a platform for the programme as a whole, would focus on a 'whole-school' approach and would carry implications for teacher training and development. Further development considers the need for small-scale innovation and development, for individuals as well as larger groups and for the voluntary and the provisional.

The corresponding issue is a responsive strategy concerning parental experience which would require a school to make a separate consideration of those areas that are of concern to parents *as a whole*, following this with a special consideration of a range of *special needs and circumstances* where separate forms of provision, or special arrangements, are felt to be necessary or desirable. Both are present in the voices of parents.

Styles of communication and relationship

Schools can adopt widely differing stances to the way in which they relate to their parents; each is born of a characteristic philosophy and attitudes which shape, in turn, its own forms and activities.

Most parts of the education service now acknowledge their

obligation to *inform* parents about the life and work of their school, college, nursery, etc. As well as being a legal requirement for schools, this has long been the mainstay of 'official' views of family/education relationships, and the foundation of home/school policy and practice. Such a stance requires little direct contact with, or responsiveness to, the views and behaviour of parents. As a result, a number of studies (including ours) have shown significant areas of mismatch between teacher views of parents' needs and parents' own views.

A commitment to *consultation/participation*, however, whilst acknowledging the responsibility of schools and teachers to lead and manage home/school affairs, also recognises the need, in varying degrees, to be responsive to parental views and experience. Participation may be welcomed, but largely on the school's terms and within existing ways of doing things; the views of parents may be sought, but often in a stage-managed way, as a means of confirming pre-determined policies and arrangements. Of course things do not always turn out as they have been planned!

Still further along this route, though very much within practical reach, is the style characterised by *joint partnership*, which acknowledges not only the right but the *value* of parents taking a full and active part in their children's education and development, on equal terms, albeit in different ways.

It is to such a partnership that we have ourselves become committed and which, for us, is the fullest practicable realisation of the strategy of 'listening to parents'. It is also, as earlier chapters show, easier to pay lip service to, than to achieve, even with honest intentions and a constructive approach. It is the task of the rest of this chapter to show how such intentions can be turned into effective action.

LISTENING TO PARENTS: A KEY STRATEGY IN THE PLANNING, ORGANISATION AND EVALUATION OF HOME/SCHOOL PROGRAMMES

Developing an effective home/school strategy of the kind we have outlined,

(i) Acknowledges the value and importance of parents in the school's overall *philosophy* based upon

• their right to be involved in their children's education and development;

• the positive benefits achieved through their active support for the life and work of the school in general, and for their children's learning in particular;

• recognition of the resources of knowledge, skill and experience that parents have to offer, which we have often illustrated in our studies of parental experience in Part Two.

(ii) Requires an honest examination of the extent to which parents are involved in

• the *planning* of the home/school programme, in influencing its short- and longer-term goals, its priorities, key forms and areas of growth and development;

• the *organisation* of home/school activities, including not only parental participation and involvement in school initiatives, but genuinely co-operative and parent-led activities;

• the *critical review* of existing arrangements and relationships and the *evaluation* of their effectiveness, in order that improvements can be identified and progress made.

In the following pages we offer a number of starting-points from which readers can begin to review home/school links in their own institutions and to develop a sense of their strengths and weaknesses. Here, emphasis is given to a consideration of home/school thinking and activity *as a whole*, as opposed to the detailed consideration of key forms and particular situations which follows on from this.

The range, scope and variety of home/school links

Teachers with whom we have worked have found the framework shown in Figure 8.1 useful in thinking about the *range* of activities in their schools; it can serve as a reminder or a map of the variety of contacts that exist and are effective, as well as indicating gaps and limitations. Secondly, it serves as a healthy reminder that home/school links can serve a very broad range of purposes. Parents, like teachers, have widely differing, sometimes contradictory, views about how far they should go in the direction of sharing both responsibility and effort. So parents will be sending out different messages about how far, and in what ways, they wish to be involved.

The framework also serves as a reminder of the relationship between purpose and form. The same practice can be used to achieve different ends; conversely, the same goals can usually be achieved by different means. So, for instance, home visits can be used as a

Figure 8.1: Towards a partnership with parents

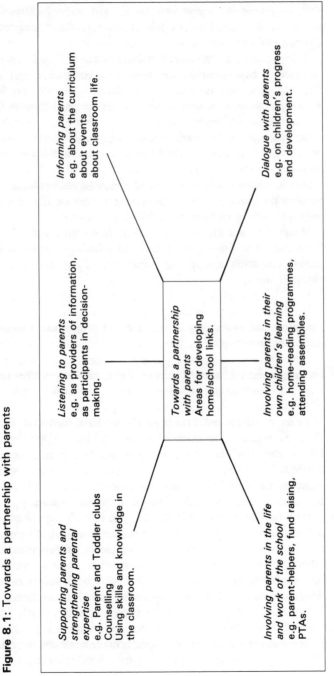

Towards a partnership with parents
Areas for developing home/school links.

Informing parents
e.g. about the curriculum about events about classroom life.

Dialogue with parents
e.g. on children's progress and development.

Listening to parents
e.g. as providers of information, as participants in decision-making.

Involving parents in their own children's learning
e.g. home-reading programmes, attending assembles.

Supporting parents and strengthening parental expertise
e.g. Parent and Toddler clubs Counselling Using skills and knowledge in the classroom.

Involving parents in the life and work of the school
e.g. parent-helpers, fund raising, PTAs.

way of getting to know new pupils and their families. More frequently it is used as a crisis measure in the management of difficult children, which is how many parents will perceive it.

Finally, such a framework enables discussion of home/school strategies which recognise the need to respond differently to the stage of development which individual schools have reached in working with their parents. This includes the need to identify:

Basic areas for home/school links, which are almost universal, either as a result of legal requirements or through 'custom and practice', e.g. written information for new parents, parent/teacher interviews to review the progress of individual pupils.

Areas where practice is *becoming established*, widespread and entering the orthodoxy, e.g. parental support for children's reading, help with school clubs and out-of-school activities.

Areas that are characteristic of a *wider relationship* between home and school, through a community school role or in the provision of education in a special social setting, e.g. family sessions, outreach work.

Planning and evaluating a home/school programme: some questions to consider

Framing a series of specific, answerable questions can often provide a basis for educational planning and evaluation which avoids much of the rigidity of an 'objectives approach'.

In the questions listed on page 111 we have tried to incorporate the need to plan as an essential antidote to many aspects of school life — the problem of too many things going on at once, the emphasis upon short-term survival rather than long-term development and the tunnel vision induced by both of these. A broad plan, by contrast, enables teachers to get their act together in a more orderly fashion, to establish priorities, to identify gaps in provision and locate areas of possible growth and development. A programme that is reasonably flexible will allow plenty of opportunities for taking advantage of unexpected opportunities, as they arise. It will also enable teachers and their colleagues to identify those areas where agreed policy is necessary and others which are better left to individual, small-scale developments on a voluntary basis. So, too, a set of clear questions can provide the framework for a critical review and the evaluation of existing arrangements and the extent to which previous goals and priorities have been achieved.

Planning and Evaluating a Home/School Programme: Some Questions to Consider

Form and style

How is our picture of parents obtained? What assumptions do we make about their interest, knowledge and skills? How can we make this picture deeper and more accurate?

How varied and wide-ranging is our home/school programme? In particular do we give enough emphasis to *informal* contact and activity, and to positive and personal situations?

How do the different views that parents have influence our work?

Evaluation and development

What do parents think about our home/school programme?

How effective, useful and interesting do they find the different elements? How can we improve the 'feedback' that we get from parents?

Are there areas where parents and teachers see things differently?

In what main ways have our efforts improved and developed in recent years?

Strategies and tactics

What are the points of growth in our programme?

As well as a short-term policy, do we also have a longer-term view of where we are going?

Are we going: too quickly to consolidate thoughtful improvement/ not quickly enough?

How realistic and appropriate is our programme?

Have we done enough preparatory work in terms of:
   staff discussion?
   discussion with parents?
   identification of resources, support, etc.?

In what ways have our attitudes to home/school co-operation changed in recent years:
   collectively, as a staff?
   as individuals on the staff?

Aims and objectives

What are the basic aims of our home/school programme?

Are the general aims sufficiently clear? Are they too general and too vague?

Are the objectives too detailed and too cluttered?

Do our aims and objectives make sense to parents?

How do we know? Do they interpret them in much the same way as we do?

How do we begin to work towards *each* of our main aims?

What are our priorities?

Scope and range

How broad/limited is our programme?

How far does it acknowledge common interests and problems?

Is it reasonable to talk about 'the parents' view'? Are there different views?

Is there any definite pattern of development in our programme?

Are there special groups who need to be considered separately? These would include working-class families in a predominantly middle-class area and vice versa, fathers, shift workers, one-parent families, ethnic groups, etc.

What special provision is required for such groups?

How far does our programme reach, and involve, parents *as a whole*?

The questions listed have been identified in order to bring out our central theme of 'listening to parents'. Their value would relate to the extent to which this process was sharpened as a result of being brought more firmly into focus.

Key forms of home/school practice

The steady evolution of home/school experience has been practice-rather than policy-led; it has been mainly pioneered by teachers and parents in individual schools, rather than imposed by politicians and administrators.

Whilst there has been enormous variation in purpose, commitment and approach between schools, certain patterns are also detectable:

- A broader range of purposes and a greater variety of practice.
- A more central concern with the *educational* life of the school. (This has brought home/school activity close to the heart of what used to be regarded as exclusively professional territory.)
- Important changes in the style of home/school contact. There is less reliance upon large-scale meetings and presentations, more upon informal, task-oriented activities.
- Teachers are less likely to consider the education of children and parental development as separate, competing activities, but as linked in important ways.

The following examples have been chosen as representative of the growing repertoire of home/school practice. Inevitably readers will respond to such a list in very different ways, according to their philosophy or circumstances. Again, the emphasis placed here needs to be upon the perceptions of parents towards these practical expressions of a school's approach and its capacity and willingness to see them as relevant to their needs and experience.

Arrangements for getting to know new families: information/face-to-face meeting/home visit.

Regular and continuing information about the life and work of the school: by newsletter/class tutor group evening, etc.

Invitations to come to see the school at work: normal routines, e.g. parent assemblies, open classrooms, etc., and special occasions, e.g. concerts, open days, exhibitions, etc.

Opportunities to review the progress of individual children and to discuss this with appropriate teachers, incorporating examination of child's work, e.g. parent folder/pupil diaries; includes regular 'formal' appointments and '*ad hoc*' visits when problems are developing.

Home visits, on a routine basis.

Utilisation of parental help and support, in classrooms and around the school, e.g. remedial work, book club/library, working with small groups, out-of-school activities, etc.

The involvement of pupils in the home/school programme.

Curriculum evenings with focus upon: areas of parental anxiety and concern e.g. maths, topic work, careers education; introduction of new subject-matter and teaching methods; opportunities to see, discuss and take part.

Development of practical support for educational activities undertaken at home, e.g. reading and language work, collecting materials for local studies, etc.

Family sessions, held at school.

Parent/teacher social and recreational events and activities.

Parent classes and groups that attempt to meet expressed needs (either directly or mediated to relevant agencies, e.g. WEA/Library or Social Services Depts).

Opportunities to join 'shared daytime classes', where appropriate.

The identification of 'special needs' amongst parents and the development of appropriate responses and provision, e.g. meetings at different times, crêche, materials in different mother tongues, etc.

Formal representation and involvement in the management of the school.

Listening to parents: some useful tactics

There is an obvious sense in which everything in this account is designed to encourage teachers to listen to the parents of the children they teach. Against such a background, the increasing contact with, and involvement of, parents and their children's schools represents a series of opportunities to develop a more accurate view of parental needs, wishes and experience. An acid test of progress in this area might be the extent to which, *in practice*, parents are becoming a familiar feature of the everyday life of schools — an accepted part of the educational landscape. Our work certainly contains many examples of the different ways in which this is happening and some of the benefits and problems that can accrue from such developments.

In this section, however, attention is directed towards the making of special arrangements that can accelerate or intensify the process of listening to parents and translate such a strategy into practical forms of action. Sometimes what is called for is the strengthening of existing opportunities and arrangements, at others, the introduction of new mechanisms and activities; at times, what is suggested involves whole-school decisions, on other occasions, small-scale and voluntary pioneering work seems to be suggested. Examples might include:

• Joint planning and task groups, e.g. to plan or re-vamp information for the new intake; to produce a joint newsletter with contributions from teachers, parents and pupils.
• Making teacher/parent interviews a two-way process, then following up their consequences.
• Trying out group parent evenings with form tutors/class teachers, to outline the coming term's work or to discuss issues of general concern.
• Developing a small-scale home visiting programme.
• Planning INSET sessions on home/school topics, in which parents make a contribution.

The 1986 Education Act (2) provides an interesting opportunity, backed by the force of law, for schools to seek organised feedback from their parents, via the combination of an annual governors' report and its discussion at an annual meeting of parents.

In addition to these illustrations of the ways in which listening to parents can be operationalised, there are a number of tactical measures that can be taken which can act as a catalyst for wider change and general development. These might include:

• The creation of a post of responsibility for home/school liaison and related matters, which might include a brief to implement school-based training and teacher development in this area.
• The use of the latest in-service funding arrangements to second an appropriate member of staff for a term, to review their present home/school programme and to use this experience as the basis of a discussion which leads to the development of policy and practice.

How parents make judgements about their children's schooling

Listening to parents provides many insights into parental perspectives and experience that are of great practical relevance and value to teachers and others who work with children and young people. But this is not just restricted to *what* parents think and say; it provides an important view of *how* parents operate. For parents seek out, and attend to, a wide range of information and evidence, which they use in very different ways to make sense of and formulate judgements about their children's schooling. The summary in Figure 8.2, which is derived from our own work, serves as a useful reminder of this range and diversity.

Against such a range, however, the efforts of most schools can seem unnecessarily narrow and restricted. For there is generally far too much reliance upon the written word, one-way teacher talk and, in the secondary school, on personal grades and formal assessment.

In an attempt to remedy such shortcomings, some schools are beginning to try out a number of two-way forms of communication (occasionally involving pupils, too), such as:
• Informal parents' discussion groups, to discuss problematic aspects of children's education and development that are of general concern.
• Putting together a folder of children's work, illustrating its range and variety, for parents to examine at home.
• Displays of children's work in schools, libraries and other places, linked to a lively leaflet with explanatory background ideas and information.
• Special 'lessons' where pupils explain and demonstrate some aspect of their work to their parents, followed by discussion with the teacher.

Examining existing arrangements

Developing effective practice in the home/school field takes place in similar ways to any other form of innovation. It begins when, for whatever reason, the *status quo* is found wanting and new ways of doing things are sought. This usually leads to a realisation that new skills and different methods are required alongside changing attitudes. Here we identify the areas of contact between home and school and examine the forms in which communication takes place. The purpose is to provide a framework within which teachers can

Figure 8.2: How parents make judgements about their children's schooling

Listening to what their children say.

Getting their children to show them their work.

Examining their children's books for themselves.

Observing a child's general demeanour about going to school.

Making careful comparisons between their children.

Asking their child(ren) directly.

Talking to other parents.

HOW PARENTS MAKE JUDGEMENTS ABOUT THEIR CHILDREN'S SCHOOLING

Engaging in a discussion with the teacher(s).

Trying to puzzle it out for themselves, working from available clues.

Visiting the school — trying to pick up the atmosphere.

Watching a class at work.

Looking at displays of work, exhibitions, etc.

Examining the teacher's comments and grades on written work.

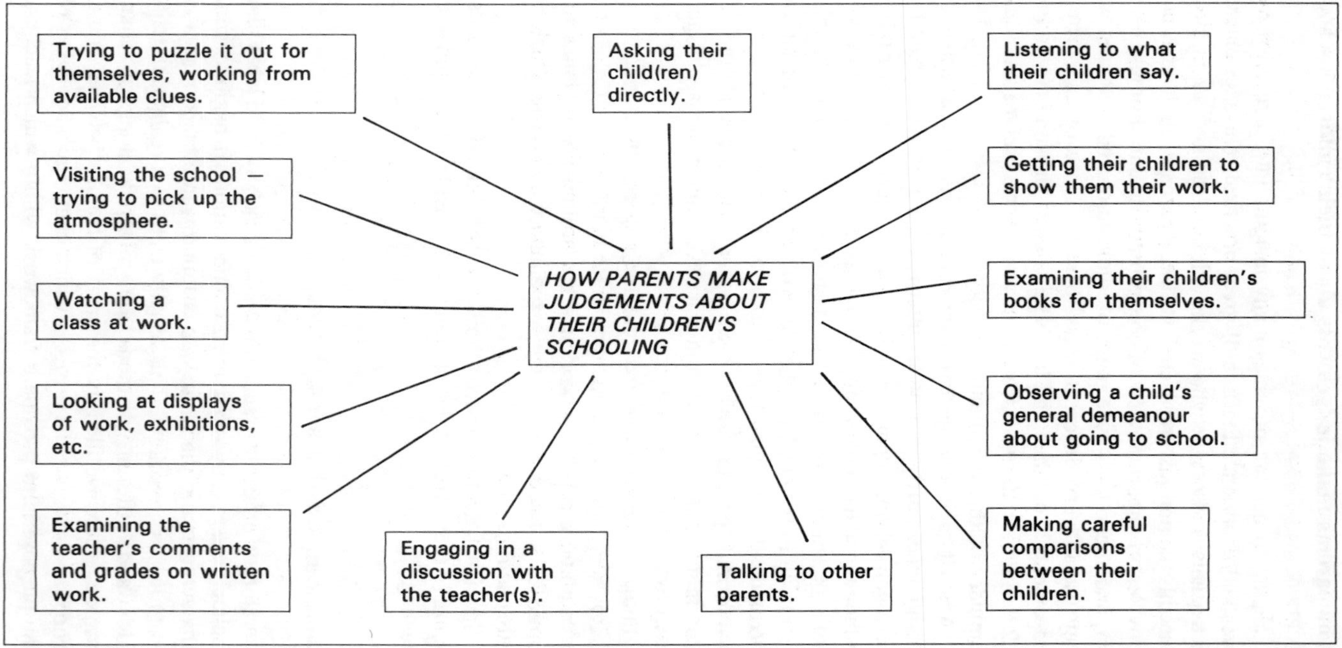

examine their existing practice and identify both gaps in their current programme and areas where growth and development are required.

However, we are not in any way offering a blueprint or model that every school should follow. While there are general themes or ideas which are applicable to all schools, the particular circumstances of an individual school (its size, geographical setting, neighbourhood characteristics, staff, age of children and so on) will be a key factor in influencing what are appropriate ways to implement improvement in home/school relations. Moreover, because we believe that 'listening to parents' is a starting-point for development, it follows that each school has to undertake this process with its own parents, although national projects and research based on this approach can provide general principles.

Our own experience, then, of listening to parents suggests that there are two themes which together provide a framework for examining existing practice and identifying areas where practice might be improved. These are:

(a) The concept of 'key moments'. It is at these times that the potential for making or breaking relationships is greatest and where the opportunity to re-establish links or forge new ones is most likely. Such moments are, for example, when the pupil starts at a school, when choices have to be made about subjects or careers, or when significant change is happening in the school.

(b) The nature of the continuing and regular contact between parents and teachers, which revolves around the progress of the pupil, the life and work of the school and the ways in which home and school can help each other.

The first theme therefore emphasises special and particular moments of contact while the second is concerned with the basic and ongoing features of the home/school programme. The importance of the concept of key moments lies in the potential there is at such times to remake or strengthen and confirm relationships with parents as a whole and with the individual family. However, it is through the regular and consistent forms of contact that the relationship is maintained. Both are important and require equal attention. For example, a school that puts a lot of energy into its primary/secondary transfer arrangements and does it best to ensure that parents are involved in the process may disappoint their expectations very quickly if there is no further form of contact until the first-year report at the end of the year. Planning the home/school programme as a whole, then, involves identifying the areas of contact suggested by both themes that are applicable to a particular school.

117

Key moments

Figure 8.3 provides some suggestions about key moments. As can be seen there are few areas of school life which do not involve the parents and any move towards a partnership model of home/school relations indicates opportunities for discussion, shared information and decision-making and joint action.

Figure 8.3: Key moments

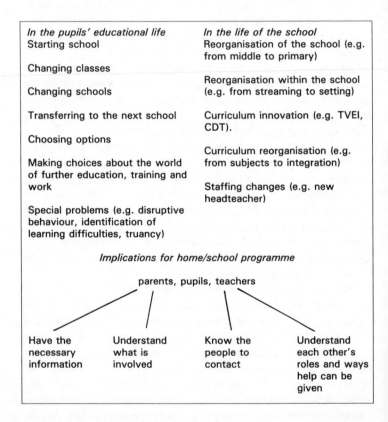

To illustrate how the concept of a key moment has been worked through in practice here is a shortened account of a primary school's strategies when children start school. (The full account is to be found in John Bird, 'Meadow Farm Primary School: The beginnings of a community school; an evaluation of the first two years', 1985.)

MEADOW FARM PRIMARY SCHOOL

Children now join our school at several points during their early years. They may join us at the Mother and Baby Club stage, at Playgroup, as a pre-rising five, at rising five, at seven years or at any point in between. We have designed a very comprehensive induction procedure to make transition into school as smooth and meaningful as possible for each child and for the child's parents, at whatever point entry is made.

We also wish to begin helping parents to develop a regular, natural relationship with school as early as possible in the child's school life and to begin the process of parent 'education'. After the child has entered school, meetings with the reception teacher continue in order to discuss our approach to learning and the parent's role. The procedure is organised in advance of each term using a prepared checklist.

The procedure and its aims

By arranging introductory visits to school we aim to:

— help the child to establish a good relationship with at least one adult
— help the child to feel secure
— introduce the child to general routines and certain activities in school

By arranging several meetings prior to the child starting school and during the following terms, we aim to:

— provide parents with information about the organisation, aims and procedures in school
— help parents to form good relationships with school staff
— show parents how to aim to educate their child and suggest ways in which they can fulfil their role
— invite parents to become involved in school or classroom activities

We aim to make parents feel part of a caring partnership by inviting them to Open Days, school assemblies, outside school activities and fund raising events.

Strategies

The procedure involves a co-ordinated range of strategies which include:

Home visits.

Introductory meetings with the staff involved.

Visits to the classroom and school.

Joining a PE lesson.

Meeting the PTA members.

Booklets on Starting School, Reading at Home, the PTA and the school brochure.

Invitations to school events before the child starts school.

Meetings on aspects of the curriculum (reading, maths and play) together with follow-up meetings.

Parental interviews after full-time admission.

The outline of one term's programme at Meadow Farm (p. 121) gives the flavour of the organisation and planning involved.

In addition to monitoring and evaluating the present procedure, the school plans in future to:

> further develop our induction procedure for parents so that groups meet regularly during each year of the child's school life in order to continuously develop parental understanding of the school's and their own role as partners.

As we discussed earlier in Part Two starting school is an occasion where the process of making a home/school relationship is at one of its most dynamic and critical points. In our opinion this school has established a planned and co-ordinated process that taken account of the needs of the parents, the children and the teachers. Most importantly, though, the programme contains within it evaluation strategies so that the process is continually being reviewed and adapted to changing needs.

Regular and continuing contact

Taking the second theme of regular contact, Figure 8.1 (p. 109) provides a framework within which a school can examine its existing arrangements and identify areas of strength and weakness. We have found that a most useful exercise is to take each heading in turn and list the specific occasions or ways in which a particular school

120

September Term

Diary of Events	Administration
Wk 1	Arrange meetings for parents of f/t chn *Approaches to Reading and Maths* (Hd & Inf/Hd Names/Address of Sept.f/t & p/t to PTA secr. (secr.).
Wk 2	
Wk 3	Letter to be typed and sent re: *Approaches to Reading and Maths meeting* (secr.)
Wk 4 Approaches to Reading and Maths for parents of f/t ch.	Hand out and discuss 'Reading at Home' booklet.
Wk 5 Playgroup Visit — Jan/p/t/ chn to join in an activity Parental interviews — f/t Sept. chn.	Arrange meeting for parents of p/t chn *Importance of Play* Letter to be typed and sent (secr.).
Half Term	
Wk 1 Importance of Play meeting for parents of p/t chn.	Arrange dates for meeting and visits of Jan p/t chn and Nursery chn. Letter of dates to be typed (secr.). Contact Nursery chn and parents (Comm. liaison)
Wk 2 Home visits of Jan p/t chn. (Comm. liaison). *Play group chn visit —* Hall act.	Distribute school brochure, free meal form, school record form, crayons, letter about meetings and dates. Invitation to Christmas prod. and Party.
Wk 3 Introductory Meeting for parents of Jan p/t chn to meet Head, Hd/Inf & secr. Also parents of Nursery chn.	Collect forms. Distribute Bank forms. Starting School brochure. Names on distribution list of MF News.
Wk 4 Jan p/t & Nursery chn and parents to visit classroom and observe. To be shown around the school. (Comm. liaison)	Arrange 2nd Reading meeting for parents of f/t chn. Letter to be typed & sent (secr.). Arrange PTA members to attend next week's meeting for Jan p/t chn.
Wk 5 Visit — Jan p/t & Nursery chn for PE lesson. Parents to meet PTA members. *2nd Reading Meeting* for parents of f/t chn.	Distribute PTA booklet. Arrange meeting for parents of Sept. p/t chn — *Becoming Full-time*. Letter to be typed & sent (secr.).
Wk 6 Becoming Full-Time meeting for parents of Sept. p/t chn.	Ask for feedback on induction procedure.

provides opportunities for parents over a period of time (a school year, for example). This will often reveal gaps or patterns which can indicate attitudes towards the role of parents in their children's schooling. For example information-giving may be more prominent than involving parents in their children's learning, or taking from parents through their pockets or their labour more common than seeking their views and opinions. As well as identifying the range of a particular programme the chart can also be used to note the extent to which particular practices involve all parents or only a few of them. What sometimes appears to be flourishing and active programme can turn out to involve only a small and regular band of committed parents, in which case consideration needs to be given to the needs of the many.

We have also known schools to use the chart as a way of monitoring their development over a period of time. By completing it at, for example, three yearly intervals it is possible to make judgements about the extent and direction of change.

In this chapter we have tried to show, mainly through illustration and example, how the process of listening to parents generates the kind of understanding and evidence that is of enormous practical value to the hard-pressed teacher. Above all, we have tried to convert our experience into forms that will enable practitioners to find simple but effective tactics for developing this for themselves.

9

Improving Communication and Contact

So far in Part Three we have provided a way of thinking about the home/school programme as a whole and a framework around which a particular school's programme can be constructed and developed.

However, central to any home/school programme is the form in which communication and contact between parents and teachers takes place. It is in the way in which interactions between them are planned, realised and experiences and how policies and programmes are implemented that the acid test as to whether intentions are matched by practice is most likely to be problematic. The essence of good communication is that it is a two-way process in which each participant can seek and give information and each attends to what the other is saying. In the words of one headteacher, though, much contact 'is like the dialogue of the deaf', in which the message is sent with no guarantee it has been received or where there is no genuine willingness to listen or readiness to hear another's point of view. Many acres of trees have provided paper for letters from school which it has no way of knowing are read, while many a parent has tried vainly to get a word in edgeways at an interview with a verbose and garrulous teacher. The instructions shown here, issued by a head to staff, are surely a recipe for just such a 'dialogue of the deaf'!

PARENTS NEXT WEEK

Further to my earlier recommendations —
Please will you

1. make a good preparation of *what* information you wish to transmit;
2. do this in your usual way if you have an efficient one — otherwise *prepare* a book page or a card for each child;
3. list the GOOD things *first*, then one or two improvements you'd like to see;
4. make sure you are able to indicate where the child is at in maths, etc.
    e.g. has learned U, V, and W *well* —
        is going to do X, Y, and Z *next*.
5. *Then*, and then only, let the parent in on the conversation. It's important that a parent should *hear* all the above. Many tend to 'run down' the children — *you* need to counter this by leading the interview.

This extract from the beginning of a teacher/parent interview illustrates what such a dialogue is like in practice.

> *Teacher*. Would you like to come in? I'm already behind time I'm afraid.
>
> *Mother*. . . . without me . . .
>
> *Teacher*. I've got his current books here. I'm really pleased with him actually. You know, since I spoke to you about him going off into a little daydream, he's, he's really trying hard. Mrs Jones mentioned to you about (*M*. Yes.) the . . . (*M*. He didn't want me to tell you, you see.) No, no, I can understand that. (*M*. You know how they like to get about . . .) Yes. I, I wished that you had (*M*. Yeah.) because I was very much afraid that I might've upset him unneed . . . (*M*. Yeah.) you know, unnecessarily. He's a lot better now because I w-was nagging him, (*M*. Yeah.) literally, because he was always, (*M*. Yeah.) *but* he's he's not now, he's coming to me and saying: 'Look, I've done two jobs, I've got on with my third job' (*M*. Yeah.) and, he's working very well. He's very, very sharp at maths. (*pause*) I'm quite pleased with his maths. (*M*. Yeah, Mrs Smith said that before.) Yes, er, all his other books are outside. This is (*M*. Yeah.) the book he's doing at the moment which is counting. It's nice and neat as well. He's very quick

you see, and there's not many corrections. And it's quite hard, they have to, add across and put in the space (*M.* Yeah.) the number that'll make it up to this one, which is just another way of addition (*M.* Yeah.). We do it in as many different ways as possible, and he's *really* quick, so I'm pleased about that. He's very quiet about it, (*M.* Mm.) he goes off and he *does* his maths without any bother at all. Now previously, with his writing, you would always know whereabouts in the room he was, (*M.* Yeah. Mmmm.) 'cos you could hear the giggle. (*M.* Yeah) You know, and there'd be a whole disturbed table (*M.* Yeah.) because he'd be there and, but that's stopped, and, erm, so I think it was worth my while speaking to you about it 'cos you've obviously spoken to him about it. (*M.* Yeah.) (*joint laughter*) Right, and erm, this, it's not very beautifully presented but there's ever such a lot of it, and it's *interesting* you see. He (*M.* Yeah.) writes a nice story. It goes on a bit. He (*M.* Yeah, yeah.) repeats himself, he rams the point home, (*joint laughter*) you know, he makes sure you know what he's getting at, but, and it's getting neater, 'cos I had a little go, you know, this is all squeezed up poorly and I asked, I also said that if he spaced it nicely, he wouldn't quite need to write that much, (*M.* Yeah.) (*joint laughter*) and he twigged straight away, and you see there's an improvement there, and I'm, I'm really pleased, I mean, every day it's a bit better. This is yesterday. And I, I can see the improvement there.

Schools that wish to develop more effective relationships with parents have to communicate not only *to* parents but *with* them as well. They have to give information but they also need to take steps to enable parents to express their viewpoints, ask questions and make comments, in other words they have to create a situation in which dialogue between listeners can take place.

Any form of communication is more likely to be successful if attention is given to the following factors:

(a) Motivation to attend to the message. This may range from thinking about style and layout in written communication to understanding the dynamics of personal interaction, particularly when strong feelings are aroused. An angry parent may need to express such feelings before being able to listen to the school's point of view.

(b) The context in which the communication is placed. Although the idea that the medium is the message is commonplace, its

The Medium is the Message

The influence of context upon communications. Some parental viewpoints.

Mother. You arrived and you would sit and you would sit . . . It wasn't satisfactory, was it David?

Father. No the class would be, all the children's books would be out and the place would be milling with parents and there was no, sort of . . . (*M.* Privacy.) The teacher sort of looked around and thought, 'Perhaps you were next, or you were next' and you'd sit around saying, 'After you' and getting more and more furious. And if you had three children, you were there most of the night! . . . By the time you got to your third teacher at nine-thirty, you were worn to a frazzle.

Father. Open night was a right fiasco wasn't it? They've got perhaps twenty or thirty teachers and you could guarantee . . . we'd got the list of what teachers he had for what specific subjects and you could guarantee the one we wanted to see, there was about ten waiting, you know, we wasted a hell of a lot of time.

Interviewer. So when you came away from that evening what were your feelings about it?

Mother. Disappointment really because we couldn't get to see all the teachers.

Father. It was the old-time teacher interview where about twenty, thirty, parents all try and grab five minutes of the teacher's time in the space of one evening . . . it was also an opportunity to look at work that had been displayed . . . my wife did go but felt she got very little out of it, partly of course she'd been seeing the teacher anyway . . . secondly, of course, because there was a maximum of about five minutes available with about half a dozen people breathing down your neck while you were talking, which my wife felt was a rather unsatisfactory situation.

126

> *Father.* Again we were in the room, it was a staggered one [*appointment times*], we were in the room at the time, you didn't so much listen to what was being said, but you could hear how the conversation was going.

> *Mother.* It's quite different when you first go in because there's an *enormous* hall and you feel very much that you're under pressure, that you only have so many minutes with each person, but after a while you get clever about it and you begin to play the system, so if you find somebody who's not got someone to talk to, you go and talk to them, which will give you greater time later on, so I think when you first go in you're intimidated by it and we quite definitely were, by the structure of the secondary school, but then when you've done it a couple of times you become quite confident in that situation.

importance is surprisingly neglected. The quotations from parents reproduced on pages 126–7 illustrate how the way a school organises its parents' evening can be crucial in determining what value parents get from the event.

(c) The appropriateness of the form of language used. Spoken and written language each have ranges of formality and the same message can be given in many different ways. Also any profession has its technical terms and jargon and the parent will often be mystified by what are quite everyday words or phrases in a teacher's language. Such language can baffle by accident or lack of thought, but language can also be used deliberately to conceal, and many parents complain about the 'platitudes and clichés' which teachers use, they feel deliberately, to avoid direct and honest exchanges.

Despite the pessimism of the head teacher quoted earlier whose graphic phrase, 'the dialogue of the deaf', is such an indictment of much teacher/parent contact, better communication is certainly achievable, as this father reports:

It was very quickly possible to have a dialogue instead of a monologue. The teachers were much more frank about what they thought, none of this, get rid of the parent by saying a few nice meaningless things and then finish by saying he isn't getting the results — but frank speaking and listening when the parent was saying something. Then you feel at least you're getting somewhere.

Schools seeking to improve their relationship with parents and to create conditions where better communication can take place might well ask whether, as a result of our experience of listening to parents, we have come to any conclusions about which form of contact parents prefer? The answer, sadly for schools wanting a magic formula, is yes — different parents value differently different forms of contact! The hard fact is that parents are not a homogeneous body any more than teachers are. They have their own individual ways of making judgements about schools, their preferred ways of seeking and receiving information, their own standpoints on the extent to which they wish to be involved with their child's education. The implications of this are that schools need to plan a range and variety of forms of contact in the knowledge that no one particular type will suit all parents. Although this may seem more demanding, its advantage is that not only are more parents likely to be reached but also that failure and success is not measured by how many parents are involved in a particular aspect of the programme. A school that offers both written reports and parent/teacher interviews may find attendance at the latter to be less than that at a school down the road which does not issue reports. Some schools have well-attended curriculum workshops while others will succeed with informal discussion with individual parents at coffee mornings. It is only by careful reflection and by seeking the views of parents that the appropriate range of contacts can be decided upon at a particular school.

To assist an analysis of the range and variety of a programme it is useful to focus on two dimensions of contact. These are:

(a) Whether the form of contact is through the written or spoken word.

(b) Whether the contact is with the individual parent, particular groups, or the parents as a whole.

Charting out aspects of the programme in the form of a matrix along these two dimensions will illustrate range and balance (as well as the extent of the school's programme). Some practices may be difficult to place in the matrix, as not all contact can be categorised as spoken or written. Where, for example, would you place a video

Figure 9.1: Constructing a profile of the forms of home/school contacts: an example

Written

The parents as a whole		The individual parent

Brochures
Letters to all parents
Booklets (e.g. option
  schemes)
Curriculum
  documents
Newsletters
School magazines
Parents' notice board
		Reports
		Home/school diaries
		Individual letters
		Home reading report
		  cards
		Personal contact
		  slips

Class notice board
Class newsletter
Year group letters
Information for
  specific parents
  (e.g. helping your
  child with spelling)

The parents as a whole ———————————— *The individual parent*

		Home visits
		Individual interviews
		Telephone talk
		Case conferences
		Parents working with
		  their own child in
		  school

Assemblies
Concerts
Sports Day
PTA events
Family sessions
Meetings about
  curriculum,
  new plans, etc.		

Coffee mornings
Class meetings
Tutor group parents
  meetings
Parents on trips and
  visits
Workshops
Discussion groups
Parents in the
  classroom
Clubs (Toddler
  groups, Keep Fit)
Parents helping in
  school

Spoken

of classroom life which can be borrowed by parents for viewing at home, or the loan of toys or reading games? Figure 9.1 is a composite picture based on a number of schools so that a full range of practices can be shown.

Analysis of the resulting profile of a school will focus around the extent to which the picture revealed shows range and variety or rather narrow and limited forms of contact. Quite often schools are surprised and pleased to find that their programme is more extensive than they had realised.

However varied the opportunities for parents and schools to communicate with each other are, their mere existence does not necessarily mean they are effective. Simply having a brochure, open days, reports, curriculum workshops or any other form of contact does not ensure that it meets either the school's purposes or the parents' needs. Indeed some long-established features of home/school contact, such as parents' evenings, can have become so taken-for-granted that their usefulness is seldom questioned. Other, newer forms of involvement, such as home-reading programmes or having parents in the classroom, can be adopted without the careful planning and preparation done by the pioneers of such approaches. In the next part of this chapter, therefore, we take a closer look at particular kinds of contact and suggest ways in which their effectiveness can be both evaluated and improved. Because the range of practices is so large we have chosen to focus on the more common forms for two reasons. Firstly, we believe that if there were improvement in all schools in these aspects alone there would be considerable change in home/school relations; secondly, we hope that the basic principles that emerge from this detailed examination will provide the basis for reflection on those we have not included. We begin with written communication, with some general points first and then a specific look at brochures and letters. After that we look at face-to-face contact, in the form of teacher/parent interviews, meetings or workshops involving parents in the curriculum, and parents working in the school or classroom.

WRITTEN COMMUNICATION

A number of years ago we wrote that written communication was 'no substitute for personal face-to-face contact' and that view remains unchanged. However, the written word is an important complement to other kinds of contact and in many ways remains the form in which most contact with parents is sustained over the years of schooling. Indeed, in schools where face-to-face meetings are mainly dependent on the goodwill of staff, the written word may be a crucial influence in maintaining the relationship between home and school. It is through letters, newsletters, reports, homework diaries, endless requests for money and information about events that the school penetrates the home in a regular and most visible way. These materials, whether consciously or not, carry important messages about a school's intentions and practices; they project images of its life and work and they help to define the relationship which it seeks with the parents.

Since the 1980 Education Act made it obligatory for written information on schools to be available for prospective parents, schools have given greater attention to the content and form of the material they provide and examination of brochures and prospectuses in recent years suggests there has been considerable improvement in their visual appeal. However, it is not too difficult to tell the difference between material produced because of such a legal obligation and that prepared by schools with a genuine willingness to inform and explain and take account of parental viewpoints and needs. Cosmetic improvements to layout and style and the inclusion of illustrations can be seen as somewhat empty window-dressing if the underlying message is still that parents have merely a marginal role in the educational process.

The task of examining and reflecting upon the nature of the school's written communication is one that many teachers have found a useful stimulus, not only to extending and improving the quality of the material itself but to raising questions in a more general way about the school's policies, attitudes and practices in relation to parents. The practical and concrete experience of a group of staff together looking at a collection of all the documents produced in any one year, for example, or indeed comparing their material with those from other schools, enables staff to identify more general issues and areas for development. Involving parents themselves in such an exercise can also lead to the raising of aspects which teachers had not considered or failed to appreciate. In this way such an examination can lead to a reappraisal of what a school has to offer and a means of relating this in appropriate ways to the needs and experiences of parents and indeed the wider community. Written communication then takes place as an important part of the overall home/school programme rather than being a neglected and taken-for-granted activity.

In evaluating written material there is an equation of effort and time to be considered against the permanent or ephemeral nature of the communication. Brochures, pamphlets, reports, etc. are likely to be more permanent documents while letters and invitations are mainly to be read and discarded. Newsletters fall somewhere between. Clearly it would be uneconomical and inefficient to embellish some communications with photographs and time-wasting to ask opinions on the layout and style of every missive sent. Even impermanent material, though, deserves attention to language and tone. Whatever the kind of written material sent, parents prefer it to be:

clear	informal
direct	friendly
economical	personal
honest	reassuring

In the light of this, the following framework is suggested as a way of looking at written material in general.

Evaluating written material

Purposes

(a) Is the purpose of the material clear?

(b) Are too many intentions being attempted in a single communication?

(c) Is the purpose best achieved in the written mode?

Form

(a) What does the material *look* like? Is it easy to read or are there areas of print in small type?
Is it attractively laid out with eye-catching headings and attention to layout and illustration?
Is it legible or marred by production on antiquated typewriters and by poor reproduction?

(b) Has the appropriate use of alternatives to words been considered?
Would cartoons, photographs, diagrams, drawings, etc. both enliven the visual image of the material and be more effective in conveying the message?

(c) Has the multi-lingual audience been taken into account?

Are translations automatically made of all communications to ethnic minorities in a variety of languages or only a particular one? (The school brochure in English with a paragraph of introduction in Urdu is tokenism at its worst. The routine translation into only one community language will offend other minority groups.)

Content

(a) Does the material take into account the parental perspective? Does it respond to parental anxieties and concerns? Does it tell parents what they *want* to know or only what the school thinks they *ought* to know?

(b) Has the social context of the school been taken into account?

(c) Is the parent invited to *respond* in any way to the material?

(d) Are there any hidden messages in the content? Is the content in any way inaccurate or misleading?

Style

(a) Are the materials written in a clear and direct way or are they verbose with complex sentences and full of educational jargon?

(b) Does the language patronise parents?

(c) Is the tone negative and prescriptive? Does the overall message convey support and recognition of parents' interests and rights or does it implicitly 'wag the index finger'?

(d) Do the materials have the personal touch or are they sent to a nameless audience called 'Dear Parents'?

Dear . . . .

There will be opportunity for you to come to school later this term to see your child's work and to discuss his/her progress throughout the year. School will be open on a number of days between 4.30 p.m. and 6.30 p.m. and the class teachers will make an appointment for you.

In the meantime, I should be grateful if you would let me know whether you would prefer to come on:—

. . . . or . . . .

We shall try to arrange times so that parents with more than one child in school are not kept waiting or have to come on separate days, but please check each letter carefully if you are one of these, as the dates may differ slightly.

I hope you will take advantage of this offer, thus showing your child that you value the work he/she has put in during the year.

Yours sincerely,

Dear Parent,

As planned we are having two evening meetings for parents of 3rd year pupils so that you can discuss your child's progress in school with the individual subject teachers concerned. If you wish, there will also be an opportunity for you to see the class tutor and senior staff. Mr. _____ the school careers tutor, will also be present.

The meetings will be held in the Lower School building between 5.00 and 8.00 p.m. on the following dates —

> For parents of pupils in 3F,3H,3J,3L — Thursday
> March 6th
> For parents of pupils in 3N,3P,3R,3T — Thursday
> March 13th.

On these occasions pre-arranged individual appointments will not be made and parents will be free to see staff in the order in which they choose. There will therefore be no need to reply to this letter unless you are unable to attend your particular meeting and wish to be included on the alternative date.

Your children are approaching an important stage in their school lives, when decisions have to be made. It is therefore of particular value to be able to discuss these matters with parents. I hope we shall see you at one of these meetings. To ease arrangements on the evening can I suggest that you arrive with a list of names of teachers who take your child? This should save you time!

Yours sincerely,

Dear

We are holding our parents' meeting for this term on _____ at _____

We expect to have all the Lecturers in attendance who have been teaching your son/daughter.

We do hope you will be able to come and we look forward to seeing you.

Yours sincerely,

Dear Parents,

I am writing to inform you of the dates for the Third Year Parents' Evenings. The meeting for 3P, 3R, 3Y, 3M, 3G and 3H will be held on Tuesday, 6th May and for 3O, 3U, 3M, 3I, 3T and 3H on Wednesday, 7th May. Both meetings will commence at 6.00 p.m. and take place in the Lower School Hall. An appointment system will be in operation and your child will make appointments with staff for you.

As you will soon be selecting optional subjects for Fourth and Fifth Year Courses, an additional meeting will be held at 7.00 p.m. on Wednesday, 30th April in the Lower School Hall for all parents of Third Year Pupils. At this meeting senior members of staff and I will talk about the option scheme and the problems arising from it. I look forward to seeing you at both meetings.

Will you please return the tear off slip below to signify your intentions regarding these evenings.

Yours sincerely,

Dear Parents,

In July, following the Fourth Year examinations, you will receive a full written report from each of your child's subject teachers. However, it is thought that you would welcome the opportunity to discover how he/she has settled down since beginning a two-year examination course, and I enclose an Interim Grade sheet giving this information.

I am certain that you would like to discuss with the teachers concerned, the progress that has been made and any problems which have arisen. For this purpose, there is to be a Parents' Evening on Tuesday, 22nd January, beginning at six o'clock in the Upper School Hall.

In order to reduce the amount of parents' time spent waiting to see staff, an appointment system will be used on 22nd January. On the appointment sheet you are asked to list the teachers whom you wish to meet. This list will be taken by your son or daughter to staff, and a mutually acceptable time of meeting will then be made. Because teachers may have to see as many as thirty parents, we cannot guarantee that you will have appointments at the exact times you want. Completing the appointments list must be your child's responsibility.

On pages 133–5 a variety of examples of invitations to parents' evenings are shown, which teachers wishing to improve their written communication could look at in the light of the framework.

Having looked at written material as a whole we now look in more detail at the two most common kinds of material, the brochure and the letter. For different reasons these are key forms of contact. A brochure takes considerable time, energy and money to produce and therefore needs careful thought; letters, on the other hand, although very much taken for granted (and probably done with little thought), are the most frequent way in which the school contacts the home and therefore are very significant in the programme as a whole.

Brochures

Since the 1980 Education Act it has been mandatory for information on each school to be available to prospective parents and this has become generally known as the school brochure, although some schools use the term prospectus. In addition to this type of brochure, many schools also have booklets or pamphlets on special topics such as choosing options, starting school, or the teaching of reading. In this section we shall refer to all these types of materials as brochures as their length and permanent nature are common features.

Unfortunately, in our view, one effect of the 1980 Act has been that in an effort to ensure comparability between schools many LEAs have prescribed the format for the brochure intended to help parents in their choice of schools. Often with uniform covers and identical headings these documents make dull reading and confine themselves to 'facts' that do nothing to give parents a picture of the school's attitudes or philosophy. Such brochures may meet the legal requirements but they cannot contain the kind of information the parent who has chosen the school wants.

Moreover, such 'official' documents are usually couched in impersonal language which seems designed to counter accusations that the Trade Descriptions Act has been broken when the child experiences the reality! Lacking in imagination and in personal contact, such brochures play little part in establishing a context in which parents can feel involved, with a role of their own to play in the life of the school.

These documents, whether LEA prescribed or not, fall into the category which we have identified as the Basic Information Model.

Typically the contents revolve around:

School hours
Details of uniform and PE kit
Arrangements for meal and travel
Explanation of school rules
Brief description of the school
Organisation and curriculum
Expectations concerning homework
Lists of staff and governors
Tables of examination results (where applicable)

Brochures such as these make no attempt to identify parental perspectives or interests, or to understand their points of view, anxieties or experiences. In addition their role in the educational life of the child is largely seen as ensuring regular and punctual attendance and completed homework, in other words a marginal and essentially non-participatory function.

Fortunately these rather negative and critical views of many brochures are counterbalanced by the many examples of materials from schools that have made a genuine reappraisal of the needs of their parents and pupils.

As a result it is possible to identify brochures with purposes other than provision of basic information. Such material often reflects some of the important changes that are taking place in the relationship between parents and teachers. Some examples are as follows (see Figures 9.2, 9.3 and 9.4):

Brochures that respond to parental needs and anxieties

Reflecting an awareness of 'key moments' in a child's educational career such brochures are concerned with:

Starting school
Primary/secondary transfer
Choosing options
Entering the world of work

Such brochures are usually produced separately from the official information material and are very different in tone, layout and design. Frequently they appear in forms which are accessible to both the parent and the pupil and in this way recognise the triangular relationship between parent, child and school.

Figure 9.2: Brochures that respond to parental needs and anxieties

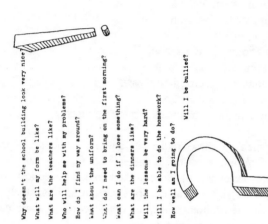

Why doesn't the school building look very nice?

What will my form be like?

What are the teachers like?

Who will help me with my problems?

How do I find my way around?

What about the uniform?

What do I need to bring on the first morning?

What can I do if I lose something?

What are the dinners like?

Will the lessons be very hard?

Will I be able to do the homework?

How well am I going to do?

Will I be bullied?

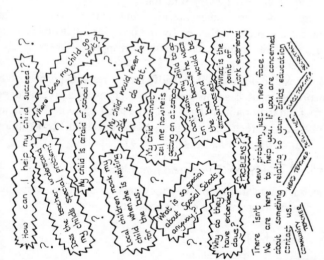

How can I help my child succeed?

Where does my child go next?

Does the teacher understand my childs special problem?

My child is afraid of school?

My child would never be able to do that.

Local children mock my child when she is waiting for the bus.

My child cannot tell me how he's getting on at school.

What is so special about Special Schools anyway?

I don't want my child to go on camp because he would be on bad and would be the only one.

What is the point of work experience?

Why do they have extended days?

PROBLEMS?

There isn't a new problem, just a new face. We are here to help you. If you are concerned about something relating to your childs education contact us.

COMMUNITY TEACHER

HEAD TEACHER

SCHOOL NURSE

CLASS TEACHER

SCHOOL SECRETARY

KIRK HALLAM SCHOOL

HELP YOU START SCHOOL AT PLAYER EAST....

Dear Parent,

We have prepared this booklet to help you when your child is ready for school. We have answered some of the more frequent questions we are asked when children start school. We hope you will find it useful. Please keep the booklet in a safe place, as some of the information is relevant throughout your childs stay at Player Infant East.

Yours sincerely *A. K. Cresswell.*

A.M. CRESSWELL,
Headmistress.

Life at School does not

Always run Smoothly.

✱ Do any of these problems apply to you?

1. My child seems afraid to go to school.
2. My child is bewildered by the work he/she is getting:
3. Does the school know about my child's special little problem?
4. My child doesn't say much about how he/she is getting on at school, and I feel I would like to know more.
5. I find it difficult to provide the money for school trips, meals, etc. Is help available?
6. How can I help my child to succeed at school?
7. Teaching methods have changed since I was at school and I'd like to know more about them.
8.

DON'T FEEL YOUR WAY ABOUT ON YOUR OWN. WE ARE HERE TO HELP:

Mrs Thompson, Community Teacher.
Mr. Hurt, Head Teacher.
Mr. Smith, Deputy Head Teacher.
Your child's class teacher.
Mrs Burton, School Secretary.

an introductory brochure for new first year pupils

"I'LL GO UP TO SCHOOL AND SEE ABOUT IT."

Figure 9.3: Brochures that initiate a dialogue with parents

عزیز والدین!

ہم آپ کو اور کو اس نرسری
میں خوش آمدید کہتے ہیں۔ ہمیں یقین ہے کہ آپ اس
جگہ کو خوشگوار اور پُرمسرت پائیں گے جہاں آپ کی
بچی یا بچہ اپنے دوستوں اور سہیلیوں کے درمیان کھیل
کی فضا میں تعلیم حاصل کرے گا۔

یہاں کے تمام اساتذہ چھوٹے بچوں کو جب تک کہ
وہ پانچ سال کے نہیں ہو جاتے۔ تعلیم دینے اور ان کی
دیکھ بھال کرنے کی تربیت رکھتے ہیں

آپ جب بھی چاہیں نرسری آسکتے ہیں اور بغیر کسی جھجک
کے کسی بھی استاد سے مل کر اس کتابچے کے بارہ میں یا اور مزید معلومات
کے لیے گفتگو کر سکتے ہیں

جہاں تک ہو سکے ہم آپ کے بچے کی دیکھ بھال کے لیے تیار ہیں
اور اگر آپ کو کسی قسم کا مشورہ لینا ہو تو آپ وقت مقرر کر کے
مجھ سے یا مسز کریمپٹن سے مل سکتے ہیں

مجھے امید ہے کہ آپ کا اور ہمارا ملاپ خوشکن
اور پائیدار ہوگا

آپ کی مخلص

S Southwell
ہیڈ ٹیچر

Dear ....

We welcome you and .... to the nursery. We know you will find a happy and inviting situation where your child will learn and play amongst friends.

The staff are all trained to educate and care for the children until they transfer to the Infant department at the age of 5 years.

You are always welcome to visit the nursery and please do not hesitate to approach any of the staff for further information, or to discuss any of the points contained in this booklet.

We are always prepared to help and advise where possible in the care and welfare of your child, and if at any time you wish to see me or Mrs.Crampton privately to discuss any problems you may have, we will be pleased to arrange an appointment.

We look forward to a long and happy association with you.

Yours sincerely,

S. Southwell

Headteacher.

We never refuse an offer of help. In fact we will often ask for your help on a regular or an occasional basis.

Regular help is needed with:

Hearing reading.
Art & Craft activities.
Sewing & Knitting.
Woodwork and Pottery.
Baking.
Brass Band.

Not everyone can help on a regular basis but can help *occasionally* with things like the School Fayre, outings etc.

We are VERY GRATEFUL for all the help our parents give us, so please......

Let us know if you can help in any way.

HELLO! you're welcome!

Teachers say "We want to help the children to learn!"

Children say "We want help."

Parents say "We want the children to learn!"

We all say "Let's get together in school!"

Come and see

Come on a trip

Let's all of us come and find out how we learn together!

Come and help for school shows

Come and watch a game

come to our next open evening

Come and read with us

make things for school

Dear Parents,
This is your school too. Come in and see us often. There's lots you can do!
from
Children and Teachers.
Blue Bell Hill Infant School.

Pleased to meet you!

Figure 9.4: Brochures that involve parents directly in their own children's learning

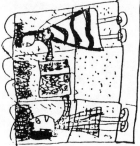

Reading at Home

Children learn

from YOU

Understanding what is happening when we work with numbers, a knowledge of basic facts and rules and an ability to know how and when to use these are behind everything we do in mathematics. We appreciate how interested you are in what your child is doing at school, but are aware that some of the teaching methods we use are very different from those by which we adults were taught. The purpose of this booklet therefore, is to enable you to help and encourage your child at home without causing confusion and worry for either of you.

Robin Hood Infant School

COUNTING and SORTING

Children can hand you cotton reels one by one, naming the colours.

Buttons can be sorted by size shape and colour.

Counting and sorting can be great fun.

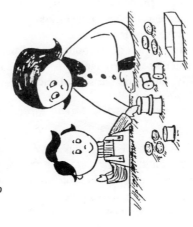

COOKING

Children love to mix, stir and weigh things. Let them help you.

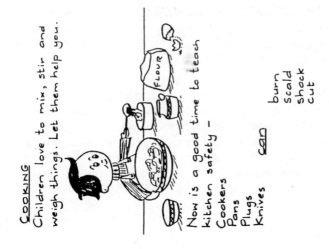

Now is a good time to teach kitchen safety –

Cookers		burn
Pans		scald
Plugs	can	shock
Knives		cut

Brochures that initiate a dialogue with parents

These materials accept the view that a partnership with parents involves more than a one-way provision of information. They form one aspect of a home/school programme that seeks to involve parents actively in the life and work of the school and in the education of the child. Such material typically includes:

* Some form of direct 'Welcome'.
* Statements about home/school relationships which contain a positive role for parents.
* A description of the home/school programme as a whole and in particular the arrangements for personal contacts with teachers.
* Ways in which the school and parents can help each other.

Brochures that involve parents directly in their own children's learning

Many schools have developed written materials which support and complement their efforts to help parents understand key educational processes and also to enable them to give practical help to their children. These brochures are very often tailor-made to the particular context of the school and written with specific audiences in mind. Examples are:

* Play in children's learning.
* Reading — how you can help.
* How primary schools have changed.
* Helping your child with Mathematics.

In general such brochures seem more typical at the primary level, which may indicate a greater openness on the part of some primary teachers to such parental involvement. It may be, however, that secondary teachers in general have not yet identified the practical ways in which parents can support the child in the maze of the secondary curriculum. Some exceptions are (a) materials for parents of children with special needs particularly in relation to literacy and numeracy and (b) accounts of the secondary curriculum which identify skills and approaches to learning which parents can support at home.

Many of these brochures have been produced with the help of groups of parents. Schools which have sought parental opinion on issues to be explored and the kind of content required have often

Figure 9.5: Brochures: some key questions

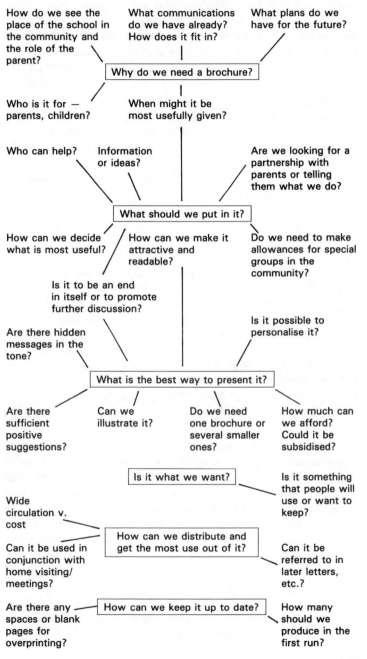

found a brochure emerges which is quite different from one which is the result of teachers deciding what parents need.

Designing and preparing a new brochure or critically revising an existing one is a demanding task but one that schools have found a great stimulus to rethinking their relationship with parents. This is particularly so when the process is shared by many rather than being the sole concern of the senior management of the school. In addition, according to the type of brochure concerned, the involvement of parents, governors, staff of feeder schools, members of particular groups within the community and the pupils themselves, in as much of the design process as possible, will ensure that it is relevant to the needs of its audience.

To conclude this section on brochures we offer a checklist (Figure 9.5) as an aid to planning.

Letters

Letters are probably the bread and butter of communication between home and school and the most frequent form of contact that a school has with its parents. Their very everyday nature perhaps makes them the most overlooked aspect of a home/school programme; from the parents' perspective, however, the cumulative impact of regular letters conveys a great deal about a school's attitudes and intentions towards them. The most carefully planned brochure or curriculum workshop with messages of involvement and participation can easily be negated by a constant stream of letters about uniform, appearance or behaviour, etc. which imply that the school's problems are the fault of the parents. Similarly, if most letters contain nothing but information about events planned or decisions already taken, claims about participation and involvement begin to sound somewhat hollow. It is likely to be in the context of receiving such letters that parents are heard to complain about the quantity of letters a school sends out. Examination of the purpose, content, style and form of a collection of letters sent over a period of time can, we suggest, enable the staff of a school to raise questions about this taken-for-granted form of communication.

It is important, for example, to recognise the strengths and limitations of letters (as indeed of other forms of written communication). They are a quick and efficient means of reaching a large number of parents simultaneously and at short notice. With reasonable care about layout and style they can seek or give information in a way which is clear, direct and available for future reference. However, these advantages make it easy to overlook their limitations. Letters sent at short notice are likely to be dictated in a hurry to a secretary when attention to tone, language and layout is far from uppermost in the sender's mind. They are often inefficiently targeted to the audience in mind; for example, a letter about misbehaviour on school transport that is sent to all parents, whether their children use the bus or not, or a single letter detailing complex arrangements for different parents' evenings for the entire school. They remain a form of communication at a distance and it requires care to prevent them sounding impersonal and official. They are most often a one-way form of contact and it is usually impossible for schools to know whether they have firstly been received and secondly understood or misinterpreted. (Despite popular mythology the vast majority of letters *do* reach home, according to the parents we interviewed.)

Nevertheless many of these limitations can be minimised by, for example, better targeting, personalising by leaving a space for names of parents to be written in by the pupils and, where appropriate, providing reply slips to indicate receipt or comment. More involvement of the pupils in personalising letters also ensures that needless offence is not given to single-parent families or children living in foster homes. On a more practical point, the amount of space allowed for replies is often an indication of how genuinely the school is seeking information. We are all familiar with a form which requires ticks in columns and gives us one line for any further comment! Better targeting, especially in a large school, could be achieved by delegating responsibility for certain letters to the class teacher or group tutor who is the person the parent is most likely to be familiar with anyway.

Analysing the range of topics that letters cover may well suggest that more use could be made of newsletters at certain intervals or calendars of events. Clearly there are many occasions (bad weather, sanctions, closures) when letters have to be sent at short notice but better planning and some forethought could reduce the number of letters on individual matters. When we studied a large collection of letters sent out by schools we found the range of topics they covered was vast, as Figure 9.6 shows.

Inspection of the lists in Figure 9.6 suggests many topics that are suitable for inclusion either in a yearly brochure or in a regular newsletter. What was also noticeable about this collection was that there was a significant overall difference in content, tone and style

Figure 9.6: Categories of letters

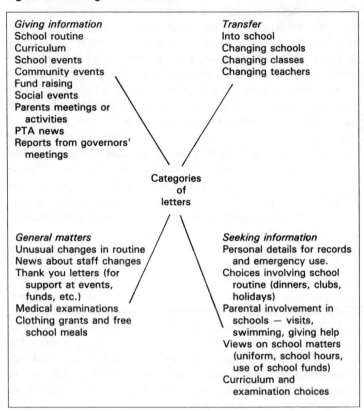

Giving information
School routine
Curriculum
School events
Community events
Fund raising
Social events
Parents meetings or
    activities
PTA news
Reports from governors'
    meetings

Transfer
Into school
Changing schools
Changing classes
Changing teachers

Categories
of
letters

General matters
Unusual changes in routine
News about staff changes
Thank you letters (for
    support at events,
    funds, etc.)
Medical examinations
Clothing grants and free
    school meals

Seeking information
Personal details for records
    and emergency use.
Choices involving school
    routine (dinners, clubs,
    holidays)
Parental involvement in
    schools — visits,
    swimming, giving help
Views on school matters
    (uniform, school hours,
    use of school funds)
Curriculum and
    examination choices

between the letters sent out by primary and secondary schools. As a general rule (although there were notable exceptions) the primary school letters were relatively clear, direct and friendly in tone whereas those from secondary schools tended to be more formal and impersonal with more complex language and unbroken print. It is easy to explain such differences in terms of the greater complexity of organisation, size and curriculum in the secondary sector. However the fact that there were examples from secondary schools with lively, explicit and personal letters suggests that a more complete explanation lies in the fact that secondary schools (again with some very notable exceptions) by and large have lagged behind their primary counterparts in recognising the value and importance of home/school contacts.

Another feature we observed was that most letters are sent to the whole parent body. Letters to individual parents are usually about discipline matters (detention or absences) or are in response to individual letters from parents. The use of the letter as a way of communicating with the parents of a class or tutor group about aspects of the curriculum (e.g. the term's project, the English book being studied, etc.) or about events within the classroom, were markedly absent. From listening to parents, we have learnt that the class focus is particularly valued by them as it is directly related to their child's current experience of school. It seems to us that the letter form of communication could be usefully exploited by class teachers as a way of involving parents in the curriculum. It bridges the gap between brochures designed for all the parents and individual explanation and personal contact.

Some imaginative uses of the class letter as a way of keeping in touch with parents that we have seen include:

(a) The use of prepared slips (Figure 9.7) which are given to all the class or to individual children.

(b) A letter from a secondary school teacher of English which describes the goals for the term's work, the way the work will be done, the particular books and themes to be studied and suggestions as to how parents can support and extend the student's learning.

(c) A monthly newsletter from an infant teacher, describing the current activities and special events that have taken place or are planned. Suggestions for ways in which parents can support the children's work are also made.

None of these examples is very time-consuming and yet in providing insight into the life of the classroom they are a way of keeping parents in touch with their own child's experiences, which is the fundamental reason for their interest and involvement.

In concluding this section on letters, we reiterate the view that just because they are such a 'bread-and-butter' form of contact, letters are of crucial importance in conveying attitudes and intentions towards parents. However, there is nothing particularly difficult about writing effective letters if attention is paid to obvious matters such as content, language, layout and design, and to the wider issues of audience and relationship with other aspects of the programme. The letter reproduced on p. 151 is an illustration of what we mean and could well be compared with the earlier examples on the same topic.

Figure 9.7: Prepared slips

MEADOW FARM PRIMARY SCHOOL

5th June, 1986.

Dear

Thank you for returning the slip to let me know which would be the most convenient time for you to come to school to discuss your child's learning.

Could you please come to school for   p.m. on Tuesday 10th June/Wednesday 11th June when we can

— discuss learning during the school year
— discuss any problems which have occurred and how they were/can be handled.
— discuss both our views of your child's learning and how we can each support it.

An important part of the evening is for you to be able to see some of the results of your child's learning in writing, drawing, modelling, etc. There will, of course, be a chance to do this both before and after our discussion. There will also be tea and coffee served by the P.T.A. in the Hall.

Please do your very best to come along. I look forward to seeing you.

Yours sincerely,

Class Teacher

FACE-TO-FACE CONTACT

However extensive and informative a school's written forms of contact with parents may be, developing a partnership with parents will ultimately depend on the quality of communication that takes place on a face-to-face basis. This is because however much opportunity for dialogue and feedback is built into written forms of contact, they remain communication at a distance. In the final section of this chapter we have chosen three common aspects of the home/school programme that involve teachers and parents meeting each other:

- teacher/parent interviews
- parents working in the school or classroom
- meetings or workshops involving parents in the curriculum

Central to these particular aspects is the educational experience of the pupil, which is the fundamental reason for parental interest and involvement in the life and work of the school. In choosing to focus on these three we do not in any way diminish the value of other kinds of personal contact — as we said earlier, we hope the general principles for evaluation and improvement will be applicable to those as well. However, if partnership is to be more than an empty word or token gesture it must mean changes in the way schools and homes share responsibility for education, which until recently was regarded as exclusively professional territory. In our view there is considerable scope for improvement and more reflective thinking and practice required before parents feel they are partners in their children's education and able to influence what happens in schools. These three areas, then, are particularly important because they illustrate the ways in which the roles of the professional teacher and lay parent are being redefined.

Teacher/parent interviews

7th July

Dear Parents,

We are holding Parents Interviews on Monday 14th July between 6.00 p.m. and 9.00 p.m. The evening provides an opportunity to discuss the progress of your son/daughter during this academic year. We hope you will be able to attend and look forward to meeting you.

Yours sincerely,

Picture the scene; it's one we all know well, though we might like to think it doesn't happen in our school. If it doesn't happen how is it we know it so well?

A big room — the main school hall perhaps or the canteen. School tables in serried rows with uncomfortable chairs for teachers and parents to sit on. Failing this the teachers are all spread out around the school tucked away in their rooms, difficult to locate and very much on home territory. Anxious parents arrive, usually clutching pieces of paper if they're lucky, telling them the time of the appointment and the name of the teacher or teachers they're meeting. Some don't have times and names, they'll have to take pot luck and try to find the teacher — join the queue and hope to be seen.

The teacher fumbles his mark book, hiding behind the columns of grades and marks. He looks confident, the parent edges forward nervously.

'Mr and Mrs . . .?'

'Smith — Fred Smith's parents.'

'Ah yes Fred . . . now let me see. Yes, a bit erratic. Marks hovering between D- to C+. Needs to concentrate a bit more. Homework not always in on time either.'

'He never seems to have any.'

'He has lots — perhaps you could make sure he does it. He'll be all right, Mr and Mrs Smith, providing he works. Leave it to me. Next please.'

A caricature? A gross distortion? A massive oversimplification? Yes of course, but at the same time isn't there a grain of truth running through this scenario?

The graphic picture conjured up by this account from a secondary school teacher sets the scene for a reappraisal of the most common form of face-to-face contact between parents and teachers. The practice of holding a meeting with individual parents once or twice a year to discuss children's progress is long-established and one that is recognised by both teachers and parents as an important feature of the home/school programme. Whether the school is officially closed to enable such meetings, as happens in part of the USA, or whether they take place during or out of school hours, as is more common in Britain, the need for a meeting is seldom questioned. However, despite its established place in forms of contact, the actual nature of the experience and what it achieves is more open to debate. Many an exhausted teacher after an evening seeing 20 to 30 sets of parents on a treadmill of five-minute appointments has wondered what useful purpose has been served. Similarly parents who have queued for hours because the appointments system has gone awry, and have spent their interview listening to reassuring platitudes or educational language they cannot fathom, have gone away feeling frustrated and unsure about why the encounter has been unsatisfactory.

Some schools have seen an answer in the abandonment of the formal consultation event and have moved to an open-door policy of being available to discuss children's progress whenever the parent takes the initiative. Our experience suggests that parents prefer a formal invitation to come from the school as this 'legitimises' their presence in school and establishes clearly the rights of all parents to meet the teachers. Placing the onus upon the parents leaves them with the problem of how often they should come and over what matters of concern. The open-door policy only seems to work well when parents are clearly informed about the arrangements and the school undertakes careful monitoring of the way parents respond with follow-up initiatives of their own as a result. One school with such a policy contracts to see parents once a term on an open-door basis and keeps records of such meetings. Parents who do not attend are personally invited and if necessary visited at home.

It seems to us, though, that reappraisal of teacher/parent interviews needs to start with examination of the taken-for-granted aspect, which is just *why* such meetings are held at all. Until the purposes are clarified and made explicit, any changes in practice are likely to be piecemeal and ineffective, somewhat like renovating an old house without asking whether the structure is sound. Such reflection needs to be given not just to meetings that are a formal part of the programme but also to the individual interviews that are initiated by either the parent or the school.

Questions about the purposes need to be considered from both the parents' and the schools' perspectives, for very often these will differ and the greater the mismatch the more potential for conflict and frustration. The following list of purposes derived from interviews with parents provides a starting-point for school staff to reflect firstly on the range and variety of parental viewpoints that exist:

Some parental purposes

To get a report on the child's progress.

To identify any problem.

To confirm existing judgements.

To find out ways of helping the child.

To see the child's work and possibly compare it with that of other children.

To meet the people who teach the child.

To bring up problems identified at home.

To learn more about the school and the teaching.

To inform the teacher about a particular matter.

To question the teacher about issues of concern.

To let the school know the parent is interested in the child's education.

To let the child know the parent is interested.

Because parents have such varied intentions it is clear that no single or simple format can exist which will satisfy them all. The open day with the chance to look at work will be welcomed by some but remain a puzzle to those who have no basis for interpreting what they see; a five-minute appointment may satisfy those who wish to demonstrate their interest but frustrate the parents who wish to discuss in detail how they can help their child. Of fundamental importance therefore will be the way in which the interview fits in with the home/school programme as a whole. Where opportunities for communication and contact are very few and limited the likelihood is that parental expectations will not be met and little of any purpose achieved. In considering the list (which is itself not exhaustive), schools might discuss what alternative methods of contact (both written and personal) would enable some parental objectives to be met.

Just as parents have a variety of reasons for attending interviews, so, too, do schools, and teachers within them have different ideas about what the purposes are and what they hope to achieve. Some of these intentions are again listed as a basis for staff to reflect on what their own priorities might be. Open and honest analysis will also reveal basic attitudes towards parents; whether they are seen as ignorant and apathetic, interfering busybodies, consumers with rights, people with particular and useful knowledge, or involved partners, for instance:

Some school purposes

> To inform parents of the child's progress.
> To meet demands for accountability.
> To establish and maintain good relationships with parents.
> To share with the parent the problems and difficulties the child has in school.
> To explain and justify the school's policies and decisions as they affect individual pupils.
> To review critically with the parent the child's experience of schooling.
> To learn more about the child from the parents' perspective.
> To learn more about parental opinions on what the school is doing.
> To identify areas of tension and disagreement.
> To identify ways in which parents can help their children.
> To negotiate jointly decisions about the child's education.

Again this list is not meant to show all the possibilities and teachers will identify many more. What we have tried to do is to enable schools to re-examine some of the basic assumptions about parent/teacher interviews as a first step towards critically reviewing the practical arrangements they make. With increased understanding about the purpose of such meetings it is then possible to evaluate how effectively the actual encounter is likely to achieve the goals of parents and teachers.

A framework for appraisal

The framework of questions about parent/teacher interviews on page 157 is intended to assist schools to review their current practice and to pinpoint areas where change or development is needed. Any such analysis is likely to be strengthened if a variety of evidence is considered alongside the views of staff themselves. We suggest such evidence might be obtained by:

• tape-recording an interview (with consent), and 'listening' to

Teacher/Parent Interviews: A Framework for Appraisal

Preparation

Purposes	Why have an interview? What is its place in the programme?
Timing	How often, how long, at what time of year? Does the time chosen enable most parents to attend?
Participants	Who is to be there? The pupil? Support staff? Interpreters? The non-custodial parent as well? What about students?
Planning	How can parents and teachers prepare for the meeting? What kind of information is needed from other staff? What work will be discussed, shown, displayed? What support material might be useful?
The invitation	Is it clear, informative and personal? What kind of layout, tone and language?

The Encounter

Welcome	How are parents welcomed? Are directions clearly displayed? What can parents do if waiting is unavoidable?
Setting	How is the furniture arranged? Is there privacy? What distractions might there be?
Process	Is there genuine dialogue? Are parents able to ask questions? Is the exchange honest and helpful to both parent and teacher? Are problems recognised and discussed? Are parents and teachers agreed about follow-up action they can take?

Follow-up

Attendance	Are records kept and non-attenders followed up?
Records	What kind of record is kept of (a) individual concerns, (b) general issues? What needs to be communicated to other staff?
Action	Is there a plan of action by parent or teacher to be nurtured? What has emerged that needs further action with groups or the whole parent-body?
Feedback	How do staff evaluate the whole process of interviews? Are the views of parents systematically asked for?

Finally

In the light of reflection on the school's current arrangements:
(1) What are their main strengths and weaknesses?
(2) What immediate improvements might be made? By the individual teacher? By the school as a whole?
(3) Which aspects are appropriate for longer term staff development and experimentation?

- what is actually taking place;
- asking teachers who are themselves parents what their experience 'from the other side' is like;
- seeking the views of parents in a systematic way through personal contact or written enquiry;
- discussing with teachers from other schools each other's practice;
- using a member of staff or informed outsider to observe what happens and to give feedback;
- recording the questions parents ask at interview and identifying patterns of concern and needs.

The framework may appear quite daunting to many teachers simply because of the number of questions posed. However, not all the questions are of the same level of complexity and in practice some will be answered very quickly and only small steps will need to be taken to effect change. However, it is because teacher/parent interviews are such a key feature in a schools programme that we believe they need fundamental appraisal and overhaul.

Parents working in the school or classroom

The practice of involving parents in the classroom or school generally is now well established in many schools at both primary and secondary level, although it is more frequently associated with the former. However, as with teacher/parent interviews, where a practice has become an established feature it is worth re-examining its purpose and evaluating experience. In this short section we highlight, both for schools that have had this type of involvement for many years and for those who are just starting or thinking about starting, some of the issues involved.

Purposes can be reflected on from the point of view of both the parents and the school.

Some parental purposes

Parents have many different reasons for volunteering their presence in school or accepting invitations to help. These include:

Wanting to get to know more about classroom life.
Wanting to be involved with the school in general.
Wanting to help their own child.
Wanting to compare their own child with other children.

158

Wanting to feel valued and needed.

Wanting an activity with purpose.

Wanting to explore working with children as a possible career.

Wanting to establish or verify views about the school or classroom from the inside.

Wanting to meet other parents.

Wanting to get to know the teachers better.

Wanting to learn more about aspects of education.

Wanting to please their child (especially the younger ones), who ask them to come in 'like other mums and dads'.

Some school purposes

Schools, too, have many reasons for inviting parents in as volunteers. These include:

Wanting to establish co-operative relationships.

Enabling individual or small group activities that need an adult's presence.

Being able to give children individual attention.

Having an adequate ratio of adults to children for certain activities such as trips and swimming.

Wanting to help parents understand more about school and classroom life.

Wanting to tap parental skills and expertise to extend and enrich the curriculum.

Wanting to help parents to acquire skills they can use with their own children.

Wanting help with tasks which will relieve the teacher.

Wanting to share with parents and other members of the community the educational functions of the school.

Wanting to get parents interested in their children's education.

Wanting to reassure or convince anxious or alienated parents that the school is 'doing a good job'.

Some problems about purposes

Spending some time on clarifying both the school's and the parents' purposes is a useful activity. From the school's point of view discussion can reveal disagreements and tensions which often stem from different value positions. For example the child-centred teacher may view parental help from the child's perspective alone — will it benefit the child? Is the parent 'suitable' to work with children? The teacher with sharply defined views on the professional role may see it as a threat to professional autonomy or as providing an excuse to divert resources from the school (a very understandable position when classroom assistants are a dying breed). The teacher with a 'community education' perspective will want to know how the parents will benefit from being involved, and will emphasise the skills and experience they have to offer. Acknowledging and accepting such different value positions is not easy and it may well be that teachers, in clarifying their purposes, have to recognise that while there may be agreement on certain issues, others remain unresolved for the time being. Certainly schools that have opened their doors are well-used to starting with one or two members of staff who are willing to have a go and seeing involvement spread as confidence and expertise grow. However, clarifying purposes can also help a school to decide first what kind of activities parents can be asked to do. For example, where establishing familiarity and good relationships is seen as fundamental, both teachers and parents may be happy to work together with the parent doing routine and general tasks to help the smooth running of the classroom. The aim of helping parents understand more about classroom life is more likely to be achieved by specific and varied tasks, including observation and discussion, than by asking them to supervise a cooking group in another part of the school. Similarly, discussion with the individual parent about his or her purposes will provide pointers towards the most appropriate kind of activity. For example, parents who want to be useful and also want social contact with other parents may prefer to work in a group preparing teaching materials rather than work directly with children.

It is also important to be aware of how parents who do help in school are perceived by other parents. It is possible unwittingly to create rifts and tensions because a group is perceived as insiders, obtaining unfair advantages for their own children. This is particularly likely if some kind of 'screening for suitability' operates. There may also be parents who think teachers are paid to teach and that unskilled help will damage their children's education. Areas of the curriculum that are seen as particularly basic, such as reading and mathematics, are most often those areas where some parents resent their neighbour 'teaching' their child. There may also be antagonistic feelings from those who would like to help but are unable to do so because of work or domestic commitments, which are often expressed by criticism of 'bored housewives with nothing else to do'.

These are the kind of issues we suggest schools need to be aware

of and discuss, not just before they commence this kind of involvement but as their experience grows. They are a further illustration
that opening up schools to parents is more than a cosy rhetoric about
partnership but can increase tensions and conflicts which were
previously unrecognised or non-existent. Nevertheless a school that
takes a 'listening to parents' stance is likely to be aware of possible
areas of disagreement and to have thought through their position on
the various problems. In our experience schools that have worked
hard at the issues and have involved parents in a variety of ways for
many years consider the advantages to all concerned far outweigh
the problems.

Some further issues

Apart from careful clarification of purposes and the kind of activities
that will meet a range of purposes, there are a number of other
aspects that also need considering.

(a) The question of confidentiality, concerning, in the main,
individual children (and possibly their parents). It would be naïve to
imagine that a parent helper will not formulate views on the learning
capacities and behaviour of particular children observed or worked
with in the classroom. Teachers need to think through, however,
how they can help parents to understand that these views should
remain private and not become topics of gossip with other parents.
Similarly the parent volunteer may need to know how to respond to
other parents who solicit their opinions on a child or the teacher or
the school generally. These kind of questions are probably best
explored in preliminary meetings with the parents and in continuing
discussion. Where a booklet is prepared for helpers it seems
appropriate to acknowledge such problems openly. One such
booklet, for example, makes this statement:

> In the world, there are all sorts of people with very different
> personalities, different talents and differing degrees of ability,
> who behave in different ways. The same applies to children in a
> school. It is our job as teachers to respect these differences and
> help each child to realise his/her potential. It is therefore very
> important not to compare children and also to maintain absolute
> confidentiality where such differences are observed in school.

Another school puts it this way:

161

Please remember:

Never discuss a child's work, conversations or behaviour outside the school. It may do the child untold harm. After all, you would not like it to happen to your own child. You may sometimes see a child doing wrong, but please do not go talking to his mother or others about this. If necessary the Head or class teacher will talk to the mother about this.

Remember children are all different. Some are more able than others and some will find tasks more difficult. Encourage them all to do their best.

Moreover, even if the issue of confidentiality has been openly discussed, teachers will need to remain alert to the possibility that their trust may be abused and to be prepared to deal with such a situation.

(b) Somewhat related to the previous point is the question of which children a parent works with. Schools that clearly differentiate children according to their abilities may reinforce that process by putting parents to work with particular groups of 'less-able' or 'advanced' children. Even where the nature and kind of differentiation is less obvious within the classroom it may be subtly revealed if parents, for example, only hear the most fluent readers or only do ethnic cookery with one particular group. Even where teachers are concerned that particular children receive the extra individual attention of another adult, it is worth reflecting what messages the child, the child's parents and the helper might receive about such attention.

(c) In considering the range of activities that parents might be involved in, the question of sex-stereotyping needs looking at. At its worst some schools in asking for help suggest that mothers can only do cooking, sewing and typing, while fathers do woodwork, building swimming pools or coach football teams! As well as negating the other skills parents may have and indeed may prefer to use, using parents in this way perpetuates models of gender-specific roles for the children in the school. Similarly where fathers are involved, either at primary or secondary school, it is more usual to find them working with boys (sometimes quite specifically with boys from a single-parent family). It is rarer to find mothers expected to be with girls only, and yet the question might be why the one and not the other? Some analysis of the school's current practice may suggest issues for discussion amongst the staff and between parents and teachers.

(d) The question of preparing and equipping the parents to be able to give certain kinds of help needs thinking through. It may well be that unless there is a member of staff who can give some 'training' to a group of parents, certain activities may require so much advance explanation that the teacher justifiably feels having parents in the classroom takes time away from the work with children. Similarly there are many activities that a short explanatory leaflet could explain and describe which parents could have in advance of a particular session. Holding an occasional meeting with the parents to discuss their feelings and ideas and the problems they have encountered enables both parents and teachers to evaluate the effectiveness of their work together.

(e) While many schools choose to start in a small way with one or two teachers or in a secondary school with one department, the time will come when a more co-ordinated approach becomes necessary. Certainly as parents become more confident they will question why their help is welcomed in one classroom but not another. The position may be reached where more parents volunteer than the school can reasonably accommodate at any one time. At this stage it may become appropriate for a particular member of staff to be given the responsibility of co-ordinating policy, organising preparation and training and making detailed arrangements.

(f) Finally, many schools would testify that having parents in the school or classroom has helped the school, benefited the children, and increased parental understanding of the complexities of schooling and of education itself. Teachers in the main find their professional status admired and enhanced in the parents' eyes. However, it would be unwise to suggest that all teachers are equally competent and successful either with children or parents and opening up schools in this way will make these differences more obvious to parents. In addition, as parents become more familiar in the ways explored in Part Two, they are likely not only to become a source of support but also to ask more questions, seek more information, and possibly challenge some of the things the school is doing.

Teachers who see themselves as having a monopoly on expertise, knowledge and decision-making are the ones most likely to be threatened by moves towards involving parents in the school or classroom. Continuing discussion of the lay/professional relationship amongst staff is a necessary part of redefining the partnership between home and school.

Meetings about the curriculum

Some preliminary reflections

Evidence has been steadily accumulating in recent years that most parents are deeply interested in what their children do at school, how and what they are being taught and ways in which they can be helped with their learning. This interest, though, is diverse in character and may not always be shown in ways teachers can recognise. Throughout this chapter we have emphasised the importance of a multi-faceted approach in home/school programmes in order that schools respond more effectively to parental needs. The same principle informs reflection on the growing practice of holding some kind of meeting with parents about curriculum matters.

Many accounts of innovation in parental involvement include the phrase 'a meeting was held to explain . . .' which conveys a taken-for-granted belief that the meeting achieved its purposes with the parents who were there. Indeed most evaluation appears to consist of counting the numbers attending and some agonising over ways to reach those who did not come. It is rare to find patient and honest accounts that assess the purposes underlying the meeting and evaluation of the structure and content of the event in relation to those purposes. Including parents in such evaluation is even rarer.

However, the detailed account of one such meeting (pp. 29–31 above) showed that there are a number of issues which make such events more problematic than might appear on the surface. To start with, parents bring to such meetings established concepts about learning and teaching which strongly influence their attitudes towards what happens in school. Whether capable of articulating these as a well-formed theory or not, they have their own ideas about how children learn, the role of the teacher, the kind of experiences that promote or hinder learning and the appropriateness or otherwise of particular content in the curriculum. These ideas are often related to their own experiences of schooling and their life as adults now, together with their actual experience of parenthood. Failing to recognise and acknowledge the diversity of these 'theories', or even worse, taking the stance that 'the professionals know best' is likely to increase misunderstandings and dissatisfaction. Opening up the curriculum (which itself is a daunting and ill-defined word!) to parents, on the other hand, brings these different conceptions to light. Far from being 'empty vessels' to be given information that is thought of as neutral and value-free, parents will filter, interpret and respond to such information in different ways according to their own standpoint.

Schools may hope that well-planned and lively meetings will persuade parents to their point of view, but studies of attitude change suggest that the process is complex and that the more deeply held the views and beliefs are, the more resistant they are to modification. To illustrate, we earlier suggested that the maths evening described might well have left parents who had a deep-seated fear about mathematics (not uncommon) even more baffled and convinced they were inadequate to help their children. The parent with firm convictions about the virtues of particular ways of doing maths was also evidently not persuaded to change her mind in one evening. In other words, a single event is unlikely to achieve much; it may possibly inform at a very basic level and even reassure parents that the school does know what it is doing, but very much more is needed if parents are to understand curriculum matters and be in a position actively to support their children's education. The implication of this is that meetings about the curriculum need to be seen in relation to all the other aspects of the programme rather than as separate, self-contained one-off events. A good example of this is the integrated induction programme described on pp. 119–21 in which meetings about reading and mathematics were part of the total procedure.

Finally it has to be recognised that change is usually a slow process. For many years parents have been excluded from the 'secret garden' of the curriculum and, indeed, from schools themselves; it is not surprising, therefore, that some will fail to respond to new initiatives. Of course careful thought needs to be given to the reasons why some parents do not attend, including efforts to *listen* to such parents, but creating a climate in which all parents feel comfortable and able to be involved in ways that make sense to them, is a long-term goal that may take time to achieve.

Developing practice

When discussing written communication we offered a framework for planning and evaluation around the themes of purposes, form, content and style. The same kind of analysis could well be adapted to curriculum meetings. Alternatively the approach used with teacher/parent interviews, focusing on preparation, encounter and follow-up, is equally appropriate and is the one we have chosen to use here. In making suggestions for practice we have drawn upon our experiences of listening to parents, attending many such events ourselves and being involved with schools seeking to develop their approaches to curriculum meetings.

PREPARATION

Purposes Think through just what is hoped will be achieved from both the parents' and schools' perspective. Is the aim realistic in relation to the kind, length or number of meetings planned? Take account of, or try to gather evidence about, the areas where parents are already interested or concerned.

Participants

(a) Consider carefully whether targeting a group of parents (based on a year group or class) will achieve more than a meeting for all parents. Decisions here will depend on purposes, but as a general rule small-scale meetings that are directly relevant to the immediate interests of parents are more likely to be successful.

(b) How might pupils play a part? Many parents enjoy demonstration lessons or seeing their children on video. Many also develop an understanding of the curriculum through the process of their children explaining their work informally at home. Some schools at both primary and secondary level have tried to build on this by using pupils as the mediators and interpreters of what they do.

(c) Whatever kind of meeting is planned it is useful to have at least one member of staff whose sole role is to observe and assess parental reactions and level of involvement, and who can, if necessary, intervene to facilitate understanding or questioning. Where a multilingual audience is present, such a role is particularly important, although an interpreter may also be necessary.

Planning

Involving some of the parents in the planning of an event can provide at the practical level useful pointers to appropriate tasks and activities that might be included. It also indicates a willingness to share decision-making with parents rather than seeing them as passive recipients of whatever the school plans. It is important to

166

allow enough time for preparing written support materials, exhibitions and displays if they are part of the session. Our experience suggests that such events are more successful when the formal presentation is kept to a minimum and there are a variety of opportunities to see, to discuss and to participate in practical activities. It is also wise to anticipate likely areas of disagreement or problems and agree a policy for dealing with these.

The invitation

Is this to be written or by word of mouth or both? A lively, clear and attractive letter, backed up by posters and personal invitations, may still not attract all the intended audience but will still be sending a message to all about the school's efforts.

THE ENCOUNTER

Welcome The start to the event will set the tone for the rest of the session. How are the parents greeted on arrival and what do they do while waiting for the programme to begin?

Setting The arrangement of chairs will often signal clearly whether there is to be discussion and sharing not only between staff and parents but between parents themselves. Formal rows will signal a one-way channel of communication which may be quite appropriate for some events but not for others. (In primary schools the size of chairs is sometimes a problem and makes the case for an active session very strong if the alternative is a long stay on a small chair!)

Process Unless part of a continuing series of meetings where staff and parents have relaxed with each other, there is likely to be some nervousness amongst all participants. Teachers who are not used to talking to groups of adults may resort to 'teacher-like' behaviour. If there is a large audience many parents will find it difficult to voice questions or disagreements. Where workshop activities are involved there may be unease at appearing foolish or unable to do the particular tasks. Sometimes a particular individual may dominate the discussion in a way that hinders the process; this should be distinguished, though, from persistent questioning because answers are evasive or unsatisfactory, or because of genuine misunderstandings. Clearly it is important that as many staff as possible take part who are able to communicate well with adults and are responsive to the reactions of parents. (This is an aspect of training needs which we shall refer to in Part Four.)

167

FOLLOW-UP

(a) The kind of follow-up needed for parents will vary according to the purpose of the meeting. Most welcome additional information that they can take away with them. These materials might consist of:

- copies of the syllabus or scheme of work;
- booklets giving more detail on the theme of the session;
- suggestions for activities they can do with their children at home;
- information about published material that is available;
- information about future meetings, or ways in which they can contact staff to discuss particular issues.

(b) A follow-up meeting of staff is an opportunity to evaluate the experience and identify general issues that have emerged and what future action might be needed. If there has been an observer, whether a staff member or an outsider, useful feedback on the parents' perspective can also be given. If appropriate, feedback from parents on the meeting(s) could also be gathered by questionnaire.

Is it worth it?

There is no doubt that a well-planned session involving workshops and activities takes considerable time, effort and commitment if it is to be successful. We therefore conclude this section by highlighting some of the advantages to both schools and parents of opening up the curriculum in this way.
- Barriers between home and school are broken down as parents and teachers get to know each other better in a situation where the focus of concern is not the child's progress and behaviour.
- Parents enjoy meeting other parents and developing a more corporate relationship to the school.
- Parents appreciate the opportunity to learn more about the education their children are receiving and to have their own part in it.
- Over a period of time parents do become better informed and develop more understanding of a curriculum that may be very different from the one they experienced. They can also become more aware of the need to support the school in times of scarce resources.
- Discussion of children's difficulties with aspects of the curriculum can take place in way that is not seen as critical of a particular teacher.
- Children's homework tasks and written work become more

comprehensible; for example, parents will know why every spelling mistake is not corrected!

• Parents are in a better position to discuss school work with their children and also to help them with appropriate advice and support.

Part Four

Listening to Parents: Some Wider Concerns

10

Implications for Policy, Training and Further Development

In this book we have put the emphasis on the value for teachers of listening to parents and suggested some of the ways in which this approach can be translated into school policy and practice. This is because we believe it is at the *school* level that a real partnership between parents and teachers needs to be implemented. However, schools and families are part of the wider community and of society as a whole. Home/school relationships therefore need to be seen as a complex dynamic in which national and local developments, as well as school-based policies and practices, provide the context within which parents and teachers negotiate their roles in children's education. In this final chapter we therefore take a broader view and consider the implications of listening to parents for the educational system as a whole.

A CHALLENGE TO DOMINANT PERSPECTIVES

We begin by looking at the challenges that this approach poses for politicians and professionals who, as we suggest in the Introduction, have for too long dominated the ways in which problems and perspectives have been defined. Probably the most uncomfortable fact that emerges from our work is that parental viewpoints, far from being unanimous and narrowly obsessive, are very diverse and wide-ranging. Parents have very different ideas about the purposes of schooling, their own role as educators, the boundaries between home and school and the kind of involvement they want both in the life and work of the school in general and in their children's education in particular. Listening to parents, therefore, challenges assumptions about definitions of reality.

For *politicians* it makes belief in the unity of parental perspectives an untenable position. Fuelled by the media, there has for too long been a phony consensus that parents are mainly concerned with standards of achievement, examination results, the three Rs and choice of schooling. Some of the parents we interviewed did echo these concerns (often those who had had least opportunity to get a clear picture about what schools are doing and were therefore more influenced by media headlines); however, for the most part we found that parents from all kinds of backgrounds were far more interested in the quality and breadth of their children's learning experiences, the relationships they had with teachers, and how they could help. Nevertheless, parental value-systems and ideologies about teaching and learning are very diverse and this means that however much a governing body is widened to include parents, it is unlikely that those parent-governors can adequately represent the variety of parental viewpoints. For parents to have more say in the management of schools is an important step in shifting the balance of power from politicians and professionals but their voice cannot be the voice of parents as a whole. Giving a few parents more say will not affect the vast majority of parents' attitudes and stances towards school unless the partnership is forged more directly with them.

For *professionals* the challenge of listening to parents is to recognise the need to redefine the basis of their professionalism. Taking the parental perspective calls for new attitudes and ways of working that cannot be achieved if professionals continue to see themselves as experts who know best and who impose their definitions of situations upon their 'clients'. This applies as much to policy-makers and administrators as it does to teachers. The issue of school closures, for example, is clearly one where professional perspectives, dominated by economics and the management of scarce resources, is challenged by the parental perspective that stresses unquantifiable factors like human relationships and the contribution of school to community life. For all kinds of professionals, then, listening to parents in the context of a partnership means a professional obligation, rather than an option, to take account of the status of parents both as a group and as individuals in their children's education.

THE CHALLENGE OF RESOURCES

Redefining the role of a teacher as a co-educator with parents challenges traditional professional autonomy. Equally important though, it also raises for the whole education system the way in which schools are staffed and resourced. For if working with parents in the ways we have outlined in previous chapters is to be the responsibility of teachers, then staffing ratios and capitation allowances based on pupil numbers alone are not adequate to the task. If partnership with parents is to be more than empty rhetoric or lip-service to an ideal, the need for staff time and resources to achieve and sustain it must be recognised. Listening to parents as a strategy for improving home/school relations will not be realised by imposing upon teachers contractual obligations to produce progress reports and attend parents' evenings. For too long innovations in practice have depended on the goodwill of committed teachers or additional staffing made available for particular developments. The need for schools to be adequately staffed for their new role has to be faced not only by central and local government, but by the politicians who have helped to shape parental perspectives on their right to be involved in education. Working effectively with parents takes time, energy and commitment; producing materials to support such work needs all of those and financial resources as well. Teachers cannot be expected to take on a new and demanding role without the means with which to fulfil it.

CHANGING POLICY AND PRACTICE

Like many other developments in education, home and school is an area where practice in innovative schools is ahead of policy-making or the creation of structures that enable change to become widespread. Such schools have worked patiently and steadily for many years, realising as they do so that new problems emerge and further issues arise that cannot be resolved with old solutions. We do not suggest, therefore, that policy and practice could, or should be synonymous. What policy-makers can do, however, is to set out a basic framework within which individual schools can develop their own strategies. They can also help to establish a climate in which a partnership with parents is seen as a part of the work of all schools, rather than an option to be exercised by some. The creation of such a climate is dependent on another kind of partnership, that between

175

all concerned with the provision of education at national and local level, as well as the schools themselves.

THE NATIONAL ARENA

Central government, in particular the Department of Education and Science, has an important role in the formulation of policy and the development of practice. Recent years have seen many significant changes in legislation which have increased the accountability of schools to parents and the community at large. However, such changes have not always been supported by allocation of the resources that much effective implementation requires. Two examples will suffice here. Giving parents more choice of schooling, as the 1980 Act did, has resulted in a large increase in the number of parents visiting different schools in order to help them make a choice. Throughout the year now a member of staff has to be found who can escort parents round the school and answer their questions. Staffing schools on the basis of pupil numbers takes no account of the time this single task takes with the result that some other aspect of that teacher's role is being neglected. The 1986 Act, making significant changes in the governing bodies of schools, while recognising that new governors might need training, has left the provision of such training to the discretion of the LEAs. The same Act requires the issue of an annual report to all parents. We cannot help wondering whether the legislators stopped to calculate the cost of such an exercise, let alone considered whether the LEA or school budget would foot the bill and what would have to be excised in order to find the finance. Responsible policy formation therefore must include, in our view, consideration of the resource implications and the effect of new policies on those intended to implement them.

Central government also has an important role to play in monitoring the subsequent impact of changing policy upon practice. This can be done through funding research bodies such as NFER or universities. The work of Brunel University on governing bodies and the NFER investigation into the effects of the 1980 Act are illustrations of this kind of monitoring. As systematic, but no less useful, is gathering data through HMI inspections of schools which provide a picture of how new policies are being worked out at the school level. Listening to parents as part of such inspections is clearly a necessary part of the process, as was recognised by ILEA when setting up the investigations of London schools (popularly

176

known as the Thomas and Hargreaves reports). HMI themselves have begun to listen to parents, rather than make assumptions about relationships based on what schools say about them, as their 1986 report on schools in Southall shows.

A further responsibility in the national arena is that of initial and in-service training. Both through the setting up of the Council for the Accreditation of Teacher Education (CATE) and through the Grant Related In-Service Training programme (GRIST) central government now exercises greater control over the nature of teacher education. A national policy emphasising the role of parents needs to be accompanied by recognition of the training needs of teachers. However the CATE criteria for initial training make little mention of this, while the national priorities for in-service training concentrate almost entirely on curriculum areas. Through the funding arrangements for in-service education, central government can now significantly affect the direction of change. Although rightly concerned about the quality of teaching and what happens inside schools and classrooms, those who set the national priorities need to recognise that a genuine partnership with parents requires such a substantial change of teacher attitudes and practice that in-service education is essential. The case is particularly strong in the light of our own evidence that many teachers now in service never considered home/school matters in their initial training.

THE CHALLENGE TO INITIAL TRAINING

As with schools, where developments have been piecemeal, haphazard and often dependent on individual commitment, so the training institutions vary enormously in the degree of importance they attach to home/school relations and the way they treat the topic in their courses. Training institutions play a very important part in socialising teachers into their professional role; changes in the conception of that role and the implications for professional behaviour, attitudes and skills, must, therefore, be reflected in the way that students are trained. Relevant training in this area requires collaboration between the institutions, schools, other placements and parents themselves and can therefore demonstrate to students a partnership model of education in practice. The key elements in a coherent programme, we suggest, consist of the following:

The exploration of home/school issues, through research and study; involving elements of a taught programme, discussion and course work. An important consideration here is that there is tutorial guidance which links these elements to the applied tasks and activities.

Maximising opportunities to participate in home/school programmes during periods of school practice: this might involve the development of the present links between college- and school-based tutors. Such experience should definitely include:

— participation in parents' evenings (and other forms of communication, contact and involvement between home and school), with school guidance and support.

— opportunities to monitor and evaluate elements of the home/school programme, and more general aspects of the relationships between the school and the families of its pupils.

Additional opportunities to work directly with, and alongside, parents in a variety of settings such as schools, family-centres and projects, family attachments, etc. This will probably involve co-operation with a number of agencies concerned with the education, welfare and development of children and young people.

Apart from providing direct experience of listening to parents, this experience should be planned in conjunction with the school practices, to complement their strengths and weaknesses. There should also be plenty of opportunity to discuss and reflect upon this experience.

College-based workshops

(a) *to develop practical skills, using real and simulated materials in tackling*

writing reports

listening to parents

running group discussions

writing letters to parents

visiting homes

becoming familiar with appropriate evaluation techniques.

(b) *to develop understanding, problem-solving and decision-making skills* — through the exploration of case-study and case-conference materials which illustrate problems involving teachers, parents and children.

The main feature of such a package is that the elements are planned together, as a coherent whole, even though teaching and tutorial responsibility might be divided.

THE LOCAL ARENA

Having outlined some of the ways in which central government can support and develop work with parents, what of the role of the local education authority? It is the LEAs after all who are able to assess local needs and the particular priorities for their own schools. Through their own advisory and inspection service they are able to know far more precisely what is happening and can encourage and support local developments that are responsive to the needs of both schools and parents. Through the consultative arrangements they have (or do not have), they signal to parents their willingness or otherwise to take account of parental perspectives on the education service. Through their own in-service programme they signal to teachers the real value they place on a partnership with parents. Through the way in which they allocate resources and staff they can foster or inhibit the school's efforts to devise new strategies and initiatives.

The key elements of an effective programme at local authority level, we suggest, are:

(1) The existence of a coherent policy for home/school relations, formulated through collaborative discussion with teachers, parents, officers and politicians.

(2) The facilitative machinery to initiate local projects, support developments and monitor their effect.

(3) The provision of opportunities for INSET work and planned programmes of training, including arrangements for the release of teachers to examine their own work or develop particular ideas.

(4) Enabling schools to have access to high quality technology and design assistance, for the production of materials that support their work with parents.

(5) A mechanism for local dissemination of development work and examples of good practice.

(6) A policy for the allocation of posts of responsibility that both firmly acknowledges the importance of the task and also recognises that every teacher has a professional obligation to see work with parents as part of their role.

(7) The creation of a mediating service for the use of both schools and parents. Its functions might include the provision of advice and information, conciliation services in disputes between parents and schools and the capacity to seek the views of parents on wider issues, such as re-organisation.

179

(8) Monitoring the needs of particular groups of parents (for example, minority ethnic parents and parents of special-needs children) and facilitating an effective response to such needs.

Most of these suggestions are not particularly new or radical proposals — indeed many of them can already be found in different LEAs throughout the country. Like practice in schools, though, they tend to be both piecemeal and *ad hoc*. What is needed, at the present time, is a more systematic approach, at local authority level, to both the support of interesting new initiatives and the spread of consolidated experience throughout their schools.

Throughout this book we have attempted to illustrate the value of 'listening to parents' as a key strategy in the improvement of home/school relations. We have tried to demonstrate its value as a corner-stone of a school's developing philosophy, showing how it should become a key element in the planning, organisation and evaluation of home/school programmes and in the emergence of more effective practice.

In this final chapter we have tried to outline some of the implications of such a strategy for the training of teachers and for their subsequent development. This is, as we have emphasised, a major task, which calls not only for the development of new attitudes and new ways of working, but for the active and tangible support of the educational service as a whole, with a special role for those who formulate policy and allocate resources. It is, however, a major area of development which is long overdue.

Some Suggestions for Further Reading

Becher, T. *et al. Policies for educational accountability*, Heinemann, London, 1981

Elliott, J. *et al. School accountability*, Grant-McIntyre, London, 1981

Johnson, D. and Ransom, E. *Family and school*, Croom Helm, London, 1983

Macbeth, A. *The child between: a report on school–family relations in the countries of the European Community*, Luxembourg Office for Official Publications of the European Communities, HMSO, 1984

McConkey, R. *Working with parents: a practical guide for teachers and therapists*, Croom Helm, London, 1985

National Consumer Council *The missing links between home and school: a consumer view*, NCC, London, 1986

Tizard, B. *et al. Involving parents in nursery and infant schools*, Grant McIntyre, London, 1981

Wolfendale, S. *Parental participation in children's development and education*, Gordon and Breach, London, 1983

'The Development of Effective Home/School Programmes' Project:
Summary of published materials and available studies

Short papers and articles

Atkin, J. 'Teacher/parent associations', *TES*, 19 July, 1985

——— 'Starting school: a focus for considering the roles of parents and teachers', *TACTYC Journal*, vol. 7, no. 1, Autumn, 1986

——— and Bastiani, J. '"Are they teaching?": an alternative view of parents as educators', *Education 3-13*, vol. 14, no. 2. Autumn, 1986

——— and Goode, J. 'Learning at home and school', *Education 3–13*, vol. 10, no. 1, Spring, 1982

Bastiani, J. 'Bridging the gap between home and school', *Where*, June, 1980

——— 'Using children as interpreters of their work', February, 1982.

——— 'Going up to school: ideas for parents', March, 1982

——— 'The role of the pupil in home/school relations', February, 1984

——— 'Listening to parents: talking to teachers', *Dialogue in Education*, 2, Spring, 1985

——— 'Going up to the Big School: parents' experience of transition from primary to secondary schooling', in Youngman, M.B. (ed.) *Problems and proposals for mid-schooling transfer*, NFER/Nelson, London, 1986

Goode, J. 'The development of effective home/school programmes', *Liaison*, Easter, 1980

——— 'Helping parents to prepare their children for school', November, 1980

———— 'Parents and teachers — a changing role', November, 1980
———— and Atkin, J. 'The child as an active agent in home/school relations', *TACTYC Journal*, vol. 4, no. 2, May, 1984

Unpublished material is available from the address below.

In-service publications and materials

Atkin, J. and Bastiani, J. 'Studyguide: home and school', University of Nottingham School of Education, January, 1984
———— 'Preparing teachers to work with parents: a survey of initial training', University of Nottingham School of Education, October, 1984
Bastiani, J. (ed.) 'Written communication between home and school', A Report by the Community Education Working Party, University of Nottingham School of Education, October, 1978
Community Education Working Party. 'Teacher/parent interviews: some materials for teachers', University of Nottingham School of Education, January, 1983

These publications are available from the Resources Centre, School of Education, University of Nottingham, Nottingham, NG7 2RD

Higher degree theses

Bastiani, J. 'Listening to parents: philosophy, critique and method', Ph.D. thesis, University of Nottingham, 1983
Goode, J. 'Parents as educators — a study of parental perspectives on the process of schooling', M.Phil. thesis, University of Nottingham, 1982

Books

Bastiani, J. *Your home school links*, New Education Press, Keyworth, 1986 (Available from NEP, 13 Church Drive, Keyworth, Notts. NG12 5FG.)
———— 'Professional ideology versus lay experience'. In Allen, G., Bastiani, J., Martin, I. and Richards, K. (eds) *Community Education: an agenda for educational reform*, Milton Keynes, Open University Press, 1987
———— (ed.) *Teachers and parents: 1. Issues and perspectives*, NFER/Nelson, 1987; *2. From policy to practice* (forthcoming)